**CREATING
COMPUTER
SOFTWARE
USER GUIDES**

CREATING COMPUTER SOFTWARE USER GUIDES:
FROM MANUALS TO MENUS

Doann Houghton-Alico

President
TIA/Technical Information Associates, Inc.
Denver, Colorado

McGraw-Hill Book Company

New York   St. Louis   San Francisco   Auckland
Bogotá   Hamburg   Johannesburg   London   Madrid
Mexico   Montreal   New Delhi   Panama   Paris
São Paulo   Singapore   Sydney   Tokyo   Toronto

001.64
Hou

Library of Congress Cataloging in Publication Data
Houghton-Alico, Doann.
  Creating computer software user guides.

  Bibliography: p.
  Includes index.
  1. Electronic data processing documentation.
  2. Electronic digital computers—Programming. I. Title.
QA76.9.D6H68   1985   001.64′2   84-25018
ISBN 0-07-030471-8 (pbk.)

1234567890   DOC/DOC   898765

ISBN 0-07-030471-8

The editors for this book were Tyler G. Hicks and Kate Schein-
man, the designer was Ink Design, and the production supervisor
was Thomas G. Kowalczyk. It was set in Century Schoolbook by
Techna Type, Inc.

Printed and bound by R. R. Donnelley & Sons Company.

To my mother, Stella Houghton Alico,
my father, John Alico, and to
Jacqueline Sharkey.

CONTENTS

PREFACE

"User friendly," "computer literacy," "ease of use." Whatever the current watchword of the computer industry, the meaning is clear. Computer systems are no longer the province of "techies." The audience has changed, and a different approach is required.

The industry has been slow to catch on. A new industry is allowed some growing pains, but sooner or later childhood leads to maturity. In business, industry, and education, computer systems are tools. Like ideas, tools are only effective when they are used. It's time to leave our silicon chip Tinkertoys behind.

This book is written for those in the software industry who want to move past the Tinkertoy stage and give their customers tools that meet defined needs. Effective documentation is the key for doing that.

Documentation alone is not the answer, but its importance is far greater than the industry has acknowledged.

This book, like computer systems themselves, is a tool—a tool to be used by the software industry as it struggles to meet the needs of a changing and growing marketplace.

Doann Houghton-Alico
January 1985
Denver, Colorado

ONE

Software and Software Documentation: What Are They?

A citizen task force studying transportation in a midwestern city went to Los Angeles to look at what then was considered the state of the art in transportation systems. They returned and reported, "We have seen the future, and it doesn't work." The challenge to the computer industry is to prevent that attitude from developing about computers. *Computer literacy* is the term that has been coined to describe our ability to use computers, and it will be a key factor in coping with the future. The major contributor to computer literacy is software documentation.

SOFTWARE DEVELOPMENT

The term *software,* meaning the nonhardware components of a computer system, was in general use by 1960. It was defined as the data elements (as opposed to actual equipment) essential to the operation of computers. Such elements included programs, routines, and programming languages. Today, the popular usage refers only to programs or systems of programs forming a unit. This book uses the current definition.

Libraries of complex mathematical subroutines used on the early computers in the 1940s could be considered the first software systems.

The general sorting systems designed by Captain Grace Hopper (USNR) and her team at Eckert-Mauchly Corp. (which became Remington Rand) in the early 1950s were the next major software development.

Captain Hopper also was instrumental in developing a common business programming language, which became known as "Cobol." It was introduced in 1960 and today is one of the most popular and widely used programming languages. The development of languages like Cobol was a necessary step in the evolution of software because the constraints imposed by the logic of the programming language establish the parameters for a program. (The primary computer languages are described in Appendix A.)

Software may be divided into two general categories: systems software and applications software. *Systems software* includes the tools necessary for creating and managing applications software on the computer. It may be considered as the management buffer between the applications programs and the hardware. *Applications software* refers to programs which are not related to the workings of the computer system itself and which have an identified end use.

Systems Software

The tools provided by systems software include operating systems, language processors, utility systems, and file management systems. They also provide the means for interfacing with peripheral hardware and for verifying applications programs. Some of the tasks accomplished by systems software include translation, loading, maintenance, and control. Initially, systems software was written in assembly languages. More recently, higher-level languages have been developed for writing systems software. Generally, systems programs are written in a language allied in characteristics with the hardware on which the program will be used. For example, Algol or languages with similar logic are used for systems programming for the Burroughs B5000 and B6000 computers.

The need for systems software has increased greatly in the last twenty years with the proliferation of hardware and applications software. Standards and training have been inadequate. Systems software is the "poetry" of the computer world; everyone agrees it is necessary to make the spirit soar, but few people understand it and fewer still can write it.

Documenting systems software is as important as documenting applications programs. The procedures are the same; the content is not. Documentation specialists must work closely with systems software programmers to ensure accuracy and adequate coverage of the information.

Applications Software

Applications programs may solve problems; produce reports in written or graphic formats; maintain (update) databases; or provide interaction with users (such interaction might include computer-assisted instruction or games). A variety of languages are used to write applications programs. These languages were developed to meet particular needs based on the use of the program; for example, Fortran was developed for scientific and mathematical equations, Cobol for business uses, and report program generator (RPG) languages for providing reports from databases. Today programming languages are moving closer to English, and programs rather than programmers are initiating the translation process that ends with machine-readable code.

The most important impact on documentation for applications programs has been the change in the end-user profile. In less than 30 years, the computer industry has moved from behind the closed doors of sequestered university laboratories and military installations to elementary school classrooms and your neighbor's family room. Documentation has not caught up with the changes. As a result, we have manuals that tell us that a system is "cute and magical" or that suffocate us with "computerese" that looks as if it were written in code.

Hybrid Systems

Certain large-scale applications systems—such as airline reservations, ticket-booking systems, and on-line banking—combine aspects of systems and applications programming. Procedures for documentation of hybrid systems are the same as for applications software, with special care taken to ensure that end-user requirements are represented accurately.

Software Engineering

At a NATO conference in 1968, the term *software engineering* was used for the first time. It was an attempt to introduce the discipline inherent in engineering to software programming. At the time, the computer industry was undergoing a software crisis. There was a dearth of reliable software for the many large computer systems being developed. Several techniques were introduced for improving software, such as structured programming and hierarchical input-process-output (HIPO). *Structured programming (SP)* is a methodology that uses established logical components to build a program. A program is divided into procedures, which are subdivided into modules, which represent a unit of logical thought.

SP lends itself to verification. HIPO represents software modules by function.

In spite of such tools, software engineering is not meeting the demands of the industry. "We are being inundated in a sea of unsatisfied user expectations," one industry expert wrote in a paper presented at the 1983 National Computer Conference. Problems include few trained professionals, poorly conceived or incomplete methodologies, and inadequate standards.

A speaker at the same conference said, "If you fail to plan for the future, you plan to fail." In 1983, it was estimated that software engineering had a half-life of three years. Software engineering's future is literally tomorrow. Many in the industry believe the biggest problem for software engineering is upper management's concentration on the profit-and-loss statement, to the exclusion of everything else. This is the same situation that results in documentation's being written off as a necessary but evil overhead expense to be completed at the end of a software development project as inexpensively as possible. To create useful, usable software takes time, money, a long-range strategy, and professionally trained personnel who combine creativity with discipline. The same is true for software documentation.

The success of software engineering is crucial for documentation specialists. How do you document a program that is not very good to start with? The best documentation cannot cover up program deficiencies. It is important for documentation departments to support quality software engineering. Assistance can be provided by creating temporary documentation for prototype systems; adapting the concept of style guides to systems programming and even to aspects of computer system architecture (which describe the hardware characteristics relevant to software development); and participating as a project team member in program development.

Development Patterns

Improvements have come slowly. It has only been in the 1980s that software development has begun to catch up with hardware development. Fast-paced hardware changes, a lack of standards, poor management, sloppy programming, and software complexity have plagued software development. But improvements are absolutely necessary. In 1966 there were about 45 vendors selling approximately 100 software packages. In 1980 there were more than 6000 vendors (not counting all the individuals writing software as a hobby) selling more than 15,000 packages. And in 1983, Softsel reported more than 12,000 software producers (companies and independents). One business forecast expects the market for appli-

EXHIBIT 1-1

U.S. Data Processing Industry Expenditures

Year	Expenditure (billions of 1970 $)	% of GNP
1970	21	2.1
1975	41	3.2
1980	82	5.2
1985 (est.)	164	8.3

Reprinted from *Software Engineering Technical Committee Newsletter,* May 1983. An Institute of Electrical and Electronic Engineers (IEEE) publication.

cations software to grow 32 percent a year through 1985. Exhibit 1-1 compares the expenditures in the U.S. data processing industry for four years: 1970, 1975, 1980, and 1985. In 1981, 1 million U.S. households had home computers; by 1985, that number is expected to hit 10 million. One microcomputer program (VisiCalc), popular in the early 1980s, reportedly was selling 20,000 units per month in the first quarter of 1983.

Not surprisingly, one major software trend is the creation of more packages for microcomputers. Development trends for micro software include more packages that are portable from one brand of hardware and operating system to another, integrated packages (database management, spreadsheets, word processing, and graphics, for example); and executive work station packages that are compatible with larger minicomputers or mainframes.

APPLICATIONS SOFTWARE CATEGORIES

Applications software may be categorized by its end use, the size of the hardware on which it may be run, or a key element of its design. End-use categories include the following:

1 Artificial intelligence (the most common form of which is robotics)

2 Business (such as word processing, calculations, accounting, and record keeping)

3 Financial analysis (such as forecasting and spreadsheets)

4 Communications (including networks, electronic mail, and telecommunications)

5 Graphics and design

6 Education

7 The arts (primarily music and fine art)

8 Science and engineering

9 Social sciences

10 Entertainment

Hardware categories are microcomputers, minicomputers, or mainframes. The demarcation line between each category is becoming blurred as, for example, high-level micros may outperform some minis.

Key design elements include data processing systems, time-sharing systems, and real-time systems. These design element categories are based on processing timing. Data processing systems are systems in which data is input and processed, after which output is available upon the user's request. Time-sharing enables several users to access a single computer at the same time through local or remote terminals. The main memory of the computer contains a supervisory system for controlling the sequence of tasks requested by various users. Real-time systems might be called "what you see is what you get." Users are interacting with the computer and getting an immediate response. Video games and simulation models are examples of real-time systems.

SOFTWARE DOCUMENTATION

Documentation is the provision of documents for purposes of substantiation. *Software documentation* is the collection of documents that explain, describe, and define the purposes and uses of a particular software program or a system made up of multiple programs. In other words, these documents substantiate (give form and meaning to) a machine-oriented (computer) process for the human audience.

There are three types of software documentation: technical (also called "development") documentation, product documentation, and user documentation. Most user documentation is not actually documentation, which is an outdated term. The point in user documentation is no longer to substantiate the program but to: (1) train the end users to use the program and (2) provide a reference guide for more efficient program use. The term "user guides" is more accurate today.

Technical Documentation

Technical documentation provides background information on the initiation, development, and operational phases of the life cycle of a particular software program. A software life cycle begins with the development of the first idea and ends when the program is no longer used.

Components of technical documentation include functional specifications (what the program does), design specifications (how it will do it), development procedures, and test plans and analyses. The documentation serves as a historical reference source for user guides, as a project management tool, and as a reference guide for maintenance of the program. Technical documentation is usually written by systems designers or programmers. It should be started before any actual programming begins because it serves as a design guide for the programming.

The documentation specialist can assist in standardizing formats and in meeting the requirements for technical documentation. The specialist can also be responsible for establishing a technical documentation library. Technical documentation is a major source of information for creating user guides, so anything documentation specialists can do to standardize technical documentation is in their best interest. In addition, standardizing technical documentation contributes directly to producing applications software that works.

Organized and clearly thought-out development activities save innumerable headaches later in a project; whatever is neglected here becomes magnified later. Ironically, most software producers do not include a documentation specialist at this stage. Development documentation frequently consists of handwritten notes scattered in various desk drawers.

Product Documentation

Product documentation is the bridge between technical documentation and user guides. In some circumstances, it may be included in one or the other. It provides specific information on product specifications, configurations, and maintenance by end users.

User Guides

In this book, the term "user guides" does not refer only to hard-copy printed manuals but to all materials that facilitate use of a computer system by the end user.

User guides may be categorized according to function or format. The functions are training and reference. In most situations, user guides combine both these functions. Possible formats for user guides include the following:

1 Hard copy (e.g., manuals, reference cards, posters)

2 On-line (e.g., program comments, interactive prompts and menus, macro or shortcut instructions, interactive training programs)

3 Media (e.g., audiotape cassettes, videotape, video discs, other audiovisual training materials)

4 Personal (user groups, one-on-one or group training)

User guides are the weakest area of existing documentation and the most crucial for the future. Standard management practices—such as critical-path scheduling—should be applied. So should standard methodologies—such as techniques developed from learning theory and from *ergonomics* (the study of the effect of the work environment on work performance). For example, the software development plan must incorporate the timely creation of user guides, and a project management plan must be developed for documentation. The function and format of user guides should be determined by a use analysis and user profile in which several factors are taken into consideration. These include the environment, range of user experience, user expectations, and software purpose.

Documentation Problems and Solutions

The computer industry is like a puppy that has to grow before the rest of its body is big enough to match its paws. Like anything that grows quickly, all its parts have not developed at the same rate. Documentation is one part whose development has suffered. This has resulted from poor management at the senior- and middle-management level; inadequate allocation of financial and personnel resources; the low priority assigned to documentation; failure to include documentation in early project planning; failure to identify required documentation; negative personal attitudes of programmers, systems analysts, and management; lack of development of documentation methodology and standards; and lack of formal training programs for documentation specialists.

Since the early 1980s, articles in trade journals, workshops by computer associations, and speeches at conferences have discussed the problems of poor documentation. Yet little has been accomplished. Why?

It is a truism that software companies are in business to make money. And documentation is an overhead expense. Few software companies have seen their profits suffer in ways that they relate to poor, inadequate, or inaccurate documentation. Nevertheless, the connection is there. The market is changing—users are becoming more result-oriented and demanding, and competition is increasing. Documentation is starting to make the difference in purchasing decisions both in the home computer market and the business market, where time and productivity are money. The industry is starting to acknowledge this fact. When it does, the major question will be whether there are enough documentation specialists trained to do the work.

Within the industry, training programs and workshops should be conducted and guidelines and standards established. Training programs can be offered in cooperation with local community colleges, vocational-technical schools, and state colleges.

There are solutions, but only the industry can implement them. The documentation specialist can serve as a catalyst for these changes.

The most important factor in creating effective documentation and user guides is commitment from staff and management to that goal. Within a software company, policies, resources, procedures, and standards must be established, implemented, and maintained. A management approach to creating documentation must be initiated, and review procedures and documentation libraries must be set up. Chapter 2 presents detailed information on the management of documentation projects, and later chapters demonstrate how to complete successfully the various components of creating user guides.

TWO

Documentation Project Management

"No particular results then, but only an attitude of orientation, is what the pragmatic method means. The attitude of looking away from first things, principles, 'categories,' supposed necessities; and of looking toward last things, fruits, consequences, facts." So commented William James in 1907 in a lecture on pragmatism. This "attitude of orientation" is what is needed for effective documentation project management. Today, the software program is the "first thing," the users the last. If the users become the focus of the "attitude of orientation," the project is on its way to success.

DOCUMENTATION METHODOLOGY

Rules and standards for creating documentation must be flexible because of the diversity of documentation presentations and formats and the continuous evolution of computer software, hardware, and firmware. Nevertheless, a project management methodology can be developed that provides an attitude of orientation for creating documentation under any conditions.

The methodology must be flexible enough to incorporate changes in technology, presentation, content, and educational approach, yet provide guidelines to ensure the effectiveness of the documentation. How can these dual goals be accomplished? The answer lies in combining a macro and micro task orientation. Exhibit 2-1 illustrates this approach. The

---

EXHIBIT 2-1

Decision Process

End result	Completed user guides

Micro frame — Research → Writing → Graphics → Editing → Production

Project management plan

Resource parameters

Preliminary content organization

Macro design — Project goal

User profile

Use analysis

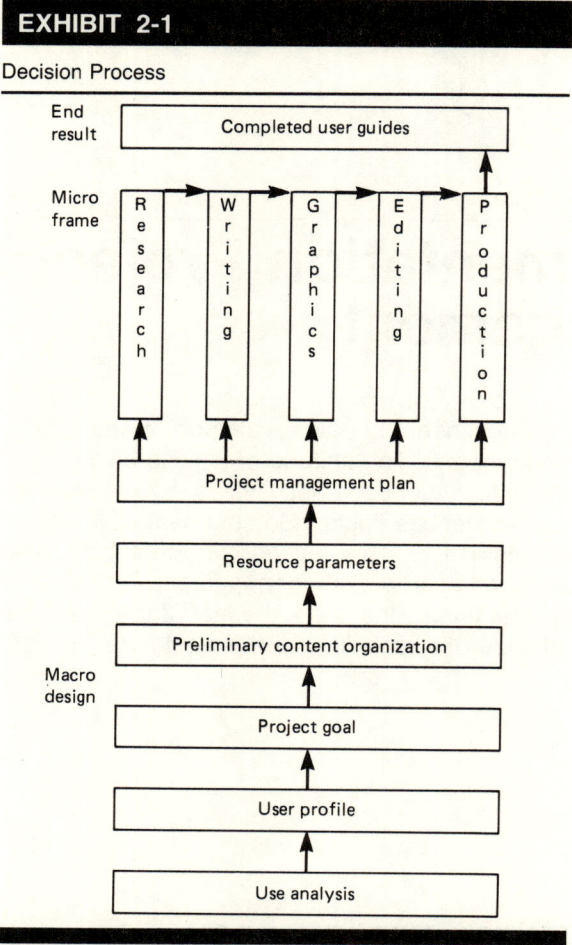

first step is listed at the bottom of the exhibit to indicate that it—and each succeeding step—provide a foundation for the creation of the completed user guides.

When building a house, the first step is to determine what the owner wants. This is followed by rough sketches and further definition of needs, which are refined to a detailed blueprint. This final design provides the basis for all that follows. The macrodesign plays the same role in documentation. The microframe brings that design into visual reality. It provides the specifics—such as research, writing, and editing—that result in a final product.

The key to the macrodesign is a use analysis, which defines the scope of the project. The elements of the macrodesign for a documentation project are as follows:

1   Use analysis

2   User profile

3   Project definition (goal)

4   Preliminary content organization

5   Resource parameters

6   Project management plan

The elements of the microframe are as follows:

1   Research including design

2   Writing

3   Graphics

4   Editing

5   Production

MACRODESIGN

The elements of the macrodesign lead from one to another consecutively, constructing a management framework. They play a role in quality control and ensure that the tasks required for the microframe are on target. Exhibit 2-2 is a sample of a documentation project synopsis form that provides a means for keeping a compact record of the macrodesign.

Use Analysis

The most important point in the use analysis is that the research should define factual data and not assumptions. Remember William James and look at the consequences. Establish a list of questions, appropriate to the particular situation, that will identify the following:

1   What is to be documented

2   Why it is being documented

3   Who is going to use the documentation (be sure to identify all target audiences)

EXHIBIT 2-2

Documentation Project Synopsis Form

DATE:

PROJECT TITLE:

PROJECT MANAGER:

USE ANALYSIS SUMMARY:

USER(S) PROFILE(S):

PROJECT DEFINITION (GOAL):

DELIVERABLES:

DOCUMENTATION OUTLINES:

ACTION PLAN SUMMARIES:

IN-HOUSE PERSONNEL REQUIREMENTS:
(Name, responsibilities, phone number)

OUTSIDE SERVICE/CONTRACT REQUIREMENTS:
(Company, name, responsibilities, phone number)

BUDGET:

COMPLETION DATE:

4 How each target audience is going to use the documentation, e.g., for reference, to learn data entry, to understand output

5 What users need to learn from the documentation, e.g., a list of sequential steps to accomplish a specific task, what system error messages mean, how to read a report printout

6 What the order of importance is of the items listed in answer to Question 5

7 What the environment is in which the documentation will be used, e.g., sitting at an input device, working at a desk

8 What factors are subject to change and how these changes would affect documentation use

User Profile

The use analysis leads to a user profile that serves as a vision of the "last things, fruits, consequences, facts." The key to good documentation is for the author to *become* the user. Put yourself in the user's shoes. To do this, you must know who the user will be. The user profile is developed from answers to a series of questions. It is essential that answers be based on facts, not assumptions. It may require a few phone calls; it may mean you have to question your supervisor persistently; it may mean a visit to the documentation user's office. Whatever it takes, start with facts.

The questions must be adapted for different situations, but they might include the following:

1   Who will read the documentation? (Verification of the target audiences established in the use analysis.)

2   What are the job classifications of the audience listed in Question 1?

3   What are the audiences' backgrounds and experiences with the software and hardware covered by the documentation? Rate this poor, fair, good, or excellent.

4   Can the answer to Question 3 change over the time the documentation will be used, e.g., by employee turnover or changes in department responsibilities? If so, revise the rating to reflect possible changes.

Once these questions have been answered, you can extrapolate a profile of your users. Write a paragraph for each target audience, listing points as needed, including the users' needs, work environment, and related information. These user profiles will provide the background data for determining the format and function of the documentation, and in conjunction with the use analysis will help you write the project definition.

Project Definition (Goal)

Now the project can be defined and a project goal written clearly and concisely. Goals must be worded carefully because they will ensure that the decisions and tasks involved with completing the documentation are on track. It is important that the goals be derived from a realistic view of the need for the documentation and not the other way around. Many project managers make the mistake of defining the project first. This is putting the cart before the horse. A use analysis and user profiles must

EXHIBIT 2-3

Sample Project Goals

"The goal of this project is to create and produce a user manual and reference guide for novice and experienced users, who will be performing data entry for the DCP Accounting System."

"The goal of this project is to create a package for end users with a variety of experience and needs; target audiences are the data processing department, the accounting department, and senior management in large insurance companies; the first two must understand and perform efficiently input and output procedures, and the latter must understand what decision-making tools are available as a result of this program."

"The goal of this project is to provide stand-alone reference material on QEDIT, an HP3000 utility program, for beginning programming students who must use QEDIT to build files and are limited to one-hour blocks on the terminal."

be completed before the project is defined. Examples of three project goals are given in Exhibit 2-3.

Content Organization

Review your use analysis, user profiles, and project definition to determine the project deliverables. What are the tasks that the software will perform for users? How do users control those tasks? This review provides a user orientation for looking at input and output. Types of user guides from which you select your deliverables include the following:

1   Training manuals

2   Reference guides

3   Audio-visual materials, such as audiotape cassettes and videotape training sessions

4   On-line interactive programs

5   Quick reference cards, posters, and keyboard guides

6   Support materials for training seminars

7   System overviews

Give each item you will be producing a working title and determine its type of content. For example, one documentation project may require a training manual for inexperienced users, a reference guide for more experienced users, a quick reference card for use during data entry, and a system overview for management to facilitate their requests for output. Information from the system overview for management may be adapted for use as the introduction to the training manual, and the training manual and the reference guide may be packaged in the same binder. Nevertheless, for purposes of organizing and writing, each item is considered separately because its purpose, intended audience, and use are different.

The next step is to prepare a draft outline of the content of each item. For example, a training manual may include a system overview, a tutorial, sequential input procedures, file maintenance procedures, sequential output procedures, error messages, a list of commands and how to use them, a glossary, and an index. A system overview might start with output, then describe what is needed to obtain that output, and suggestions on merging output to produce different management tools. More detailed information on documentation content is included in the chapters on creating written user guides and on-line documentation.

Resource Parameters

Sequentially itemize the tasks to be completed under the elements of the microframe by studying the content outline for each user aid to be produced. A simple matrix table can help establish required personnel resources, personnel time, and project costs. Also use this table to build the schedule required for your project management plan. Exhibit 2-4 shows a form that may be used to determine personnel requirements. Exhibit 2-5 shows a personnel costs table constructed for a project to write and produce a training manual for novice users of a word processing program.

Project Management Plan

A project management plan is created easily from the completed macrodesign steps, which started with the use analysis. It should be put in a graphic format on a word processor so that changes can be reflected and the plan is always up to date. There are many styles that can be used, including critical-path and matrix formats. The key is that only essential information is included. The specific situation governs the final plan, but it should include the project goal, schedule, and budget. Exhibit 2-6 is an example of a project management plan.

EXHIBIT 2-4

Personnel Requirements

Manual Sections	Personnel Time											
	Phase											
	Research and write first draft	Word processing (WP)	Revisions, editing	WP	Proof final edit	Prepare review copies	Incorporate review comments	WP	Final proof	Final WP	Production preparation (final graphics layout)	Production
System description	A/1 B/5	C/2	B/2	C/1	B/2	B/1 C/1	B/2	C/2	B/2	C/2	B/1 D/2	
Keyboard description	B/10	C/4	B/3	C/1	B/2	B/1 C/1	B/2	C/2	B/2	C/2	B/1 D/2	
Tutorial (writing a letter)	B/15	C/6	B/3	C/2	B/2	B/1 C/1	B/2	C/2	B/2	C/2	B/1 D/2	
Task descriptions	B/15	C/6	B/3	C/2	B/2	B/1 C/1	B/2	C/2	B/2	C/2	B/1 D/2	
Error messages	B/12	C/5	B/3	C/2	B/2	B/1 C/1	B/2	C/2	B/2	C/2	B/1 D/2	
Commands	B/15	C/6	B/3	C/2	B/2	B/1 C/1	B/2	C/2	B/2	C/2	B/1 D/2	
Glossary	B/5	C/4	B/2	C/1	B/2	B/1 C/1	B/2	C/2	B/2	C/2	B/1 D/1	
Index	B/8	C/6	B/4	C/3	B/2	B/1 C/1	B/2	C/2	B/2	C/2	B/1 D/1	B/2, D/2 E/45 (Total manual)

Personnel Symbols: A = documentation project manager; B = documentation writer; C = word processor; D = design-layout specialist; E = production staff; followed by a slash (/) and estimated number of hours.

EXHIBIT 2-5

Personnel Costs

Personnel	Number of Hours	Billable Rate ($)	Total Cost to Project ($)
Documentation project manager	29	75	2,175
Documentation writer	186*	35	6,510
Word processor	93	12	1,116
Design specialist	16	40	640
Production staff	45	25	1,125
Total personnel costs			$11,566

*Additional hours included for administrative tasks.

MICROFRAME

A brief action plan is developed for each microframe element. The document organization and project organization completed during the macrodesign provide the background data for most of the microframe action plans. These action plans provide management of day-to-day operations of the project and ensure that the schedule is being met.

Research

Identify the information needed, the source of that information, and required research techniques. Then establish a schedule for completing the research. This is your research action plan. Exhibit 2-7 is a sample research action plan. Research techniques and procedures are discussed in Chapter 3. Design is first addressed during research, and also in writing and graphics.

Writing

The writing of the guides and documentation is the most important component for conveying an understanding of the system and the users' responsibilities for making it work. Only an experienced technical writer with training in documentation should write user guides. They should

EXHIBIT 2-6

Project Management Form

Project goal: The goal of this project is to produce a user manual including training and reference materials for all clerks (novice to expert) entering and updating data for the DCP Accounting System.

Deliverables: 1000 copies in three-ring view binders with section tabs; client will provide cover title page.

Due date: October 1, 19___

Total budget: $32,500

Schedule:

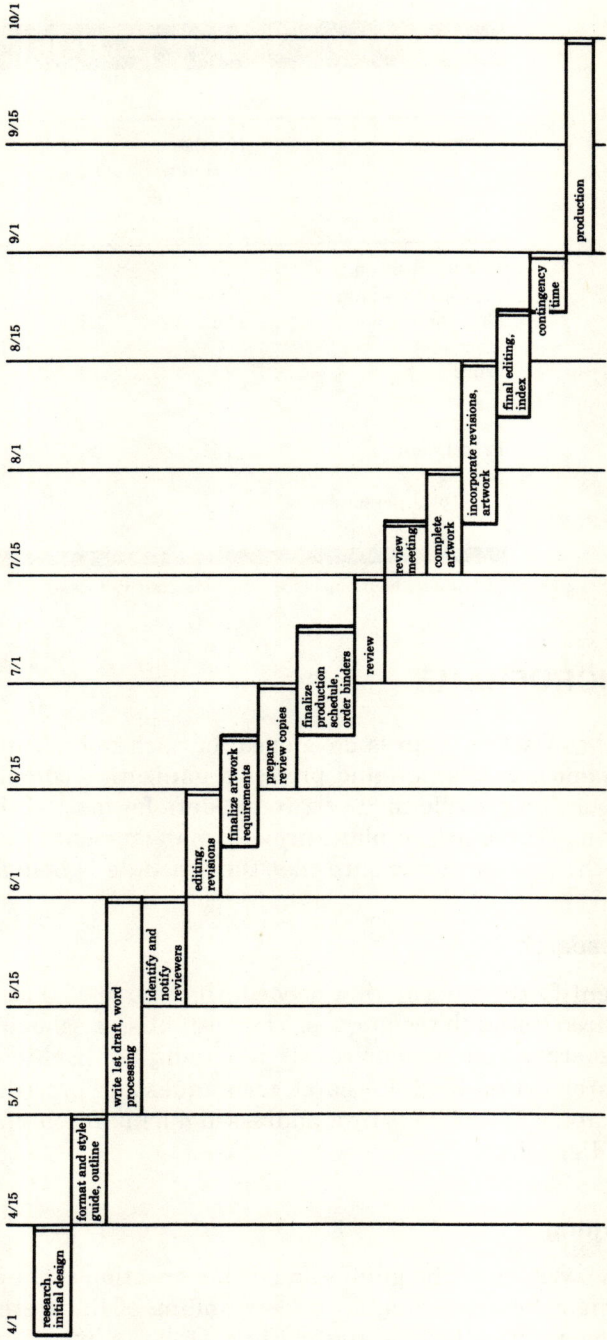

EXHIBIT 2-7

Research Action Plan

Manual Sections	Sources of Information	Completion Date
System description	Marketing staff Specs Systems designer	6/14
Keyboard description	Specs Verify with hands-on experience	6/21
Tutorial (writing a letter)	Hands-on experience	6/24
Task descriptions	Programs Specs Systems designer	6/30
Error messages	Programs Hands-on experience	7/6
Commands	Programs Specs Systems designer	7/12
Glossary	Notes from other sections	9/13
Index	Final document	9/20

not be written by programmers, systems analysts, or marketing personnel. As with research, the documentation specialist should develop a writing action plan that lists each section and subsection to be written and the date it must be completed. Time must be allocated for typing or word processing, editing, revisions, proofing, and review. The writing action plan can be taken from the schedule in the project management plan. It may be broken down into manual sections if the project is complex and if that additional management tool is needed. Chapter 4 discusses writing hard-copy user guides, and Chapter 5 covers on-line interactive user guides, including menus and help commands.

Graphics

It is essential that both the data to be presented and the end use of the document be considered when determining graphic presentations. The only effective approach is constant attention to needs assessment and to remaining on target with the carefully constructed project goals. Graphic presentations in documentation range from traditional flowcharts to menu screens, from code-decode tables to photographs of keyboards. Review the user profiles and the documentation content outline developed for the writing action plan and make a list of potential graphics. Review that list with the design and production resource personnel to determine what can be done within the project time and budget constraints. Once you have determined what graphics will be included, prepare a graphics action plan listing each graphic to be used, how it will be created and by whom (and his or her telephone number), the date by which that person must receive the assignment and necessary content information, and the due date. Exhibit 2-8 is a section of a sample graphics action plan. The use of graphics in user documentation is discussed in detail in Chapter 6.

Editing

Experienced writers consider editing an integral part of writing. User guides require a variety of editing processes, e.g., technical editing or reviewing; text editing, which must include a review from a "user advocate"; and standard proofreading. The editing action plan can be incorporated into the writing action plan, but if it is not, additional planning is required. Editing is discussed in more detail in Chapter 7.

Production

Many documentation specialists are inexperienced with production systems and techniques. Therefore, they often find the process causes what

---

EXHIBIT 2-8

Sample Graphics Action Plan

Manual Sections	Graphics	Source of Content	Designer	Telephone	Due Date
System overview	Process diagram	Text	B. Poulos	ext. 321	9/20
	Illustration/system in use	Designer	D. Haines	ext. 355	9/15
	Series of illustrations (reduc.) between sections	Designer	D. Haines	ext. 355	9/15
Keyboard description	Photo of keyboard	Marketing	J. Peters	ext. 888	8/1
	Illustrations of specific keys	Designer	D. Haines	ext. 355	8/15
Tutorial	Example of final letter	Text	B. Poulos (word proc.)	ext. 321 ext. 251	8/20
	Highlighted sections of letter	Text	B. Poulos (production)	ext. 321 ext. 242	8/25

they consider unforeseen problems and delays. The primary component of production is printing. It also includes preparation of copy for printing, as well as binding and assembling of the final user guides. Familiarity with production procedures and proper preparation will shorten the time needed for a documentation project, improve the quality of the product, and reduce the stress of tight deadlines. There are companies that take over the function of manufacturing or producing text documentation, but they require schedules, deadlines, and preparation too. In other words, there is no escape from confronting production.

Decide in advance what production system you will be using for your text or media materials, develop a contact person in the in-house department or outside firm that will be doing the work, and keep that person informed of your progress. Be sure you know exactly what format the manuscript must be in for production. Once you itemize the requirements and set up your timetable, you have your production action plan. Exhibit 2-9 is a sample production action plan. Chapter 8 discusses production procedures.

DISTRIBUTION AND MAINTENANCE

Creating the documentation is only the first step. It must be distributed to everyone using the program, and it must be kept up to date, incorporating changes in the program.

If the documentation is for an off-the-shelf applications program, it is reproduced and packaged with the program. Documentation distribution for most systems software and for customized and other applications software must be managed carefully so that accurate records are maintained.

Establish centralized records with columns showing who receives documentation, the date the documentation was issued, the date any updates were released, and whether the documentation has been returned for any reason. If the circumstances call for it, send a cover letter or memo with the documentation explaining what it covers, how to use it, and whom to contact in your organization if questions or problems arise.

As programs are updated, the documentation must be as well. One of the biggest problems for many documentation departments is finding out when and how programs are updated. The attitude of some programmers toward documentation has been one of the stumbling blocks to producing quality documentation. This attitude is changing as programmers recognize the economic necessity of having good documentation and as professional standards are enforced and programming becomes less creative and more disciplined. What can you do to bridge the gap?

First, talk to the programmers responsible for the programs you will

EXHIBIT 2-9

Sample Production Action Plan

Product	Printing Method/ Binding Process	Deliverable to Printer	Printer	Contact	Phone	Due Date	Completion Date	Notes
DCP acct. system user manual	Typeset, bound in 3-ring binders with tabs	Clean final copy, design specs attached	Bell Press	L. Bell	355-1212	9/28	10/12	Meet with Bell Press designer 9/1 to finalize design specs
DCP acct. system quick reference cards	Typeset, laminated plastic cardboard	Clean final copy, design specs attached	Bell Press	L. Bell	355-1212	9/28	10/12	Meet with Bell Press designer 9/1 to finalize design specs
DCP acct. system training support materials	Word processed, copies, spiral bound	Final word-processed original, paginated, including headers & footers for back-to-back printing	In-house prod. dept.	S. Jack	ext. 375	9/12	9/20	
DCP acct. system tech. doc. and installation instructions	Word processed, copies, 3-ring binders	Final word-processed original, paginated, including headers & footers for back-to-back printing	In-house prod. dept.	S. Jack	ext. 375	9/25	9/30	Order binders by 8/10

be documenting. Take them out to lunch, tell them what your responsibilities and deadlines are, ask for their cooperation, and offer to help them with the technical documentation. Ensure that you have management support for your tasks and suggest that memos and other direct symbols of that support be circulated in the programming department. Prepare simple check-the-box forms for programmers to fill out for you when they make changes in existing programs. Check with them periodically to see what changes are being considered and what the schedule is.

When you do have programming changes that affect users, determine what percentage of the documentation needs to be updated and the costs for reproducing the entire document as opposed to the required pages. Usually updates will consist of pages to be inserted into the original document. Be sure the new page carries a header or footer with the revision date and number of the page it is replacing. If the table of contents is affected by the updates, issue a new table of contents too. You may choose to note revision dates on the table of contents if they apply to entire sections or subsections. One method of ensuring that all users have the required updates is to number sequentially each set of cover letters accompanying the updates. Each user should have a set numbered from 1 through however many updates there have been. Periodically, send users a memo asking them to check off any number not received and to return the form to you. Be sure to enclose a prepaid self-addressed envelope.

EVALUATION

There are three primary methods for critiquing your work:

1   In-house review before the documentation is released

2   User surveys

3   Industry evaluation after the system has been in use

In-house review should be made a part of the documentation creation process, and user surveys should be conducted periodically. Evaluation procedures are discussed in detail in Chapter 7.

If the proposed project management methodology presented here is used for documentation projects, the end result should be user guides that work. But how do you know whether they work? Perhaps you have developed and implemented your project management plan and you believe all your data is accurate and your decisions reasonable. Nevertheless, you rarely have direct contact with the end users. Are they using the documents as you expected? What else do they need? What tricks have they learned that you should pass on to other less experienced users?

Read what the trade journals are saying about your documentation. How is it being rated in comparison with your competitors? Talk to the editors and find out what criteria they are using for evaluating software documentation and ask them for feedback about your particular product when they review it.

THREE

Research Procedures

There are three primary sources of information for the documentation specialist:

1 Written information, such as program specifications, flowcharts, and system design notes

2 Computer-generated information, such as program output and source code

3 Interviews with personnel such as programmers and marketing staff

DATA COLLECTION

Complete the content outline for the user guide and other documents you are creating for a particular software system or program. For most applications software, you will need to know the following:

1 Purpose of the system—how it works in terms of timing, process, and human interface

2 System entry and exit procedures

3 Data entry information—sequential procedures, content, time frame, alternatives, potential problems and their solutions

4 Data maintenance and update procedures—additions, corrections, deletions, reformatting

5 User functions—tasks to be performed, sequential procedures, interface format, potential errors and means for making corrections

6 Reference information—field descriptions; list of error messages; and unique key, prompt, or command use

Make a list for each section of all the data you need to write that section. Use a three-column format. The Data column describes the specific information you need, the Source column identifies where it can be found, and the Date column lists the date by which you want to have that information. See Exhibit 3-1 for an example.

Once these resource identification sheets are filled in for each section, review them to identify all the information you need from one source. This will provide a checklist when you are reviewing a printout or establishing questions for an interview.

Written Information

Obtain all existing written information about the system you are documenting. Insist on having copies of system specifications; relevant client correspondence if it is a customized system; flowcharts; other technical documentation; system design notes; and marketing, sales, and other promotional material. Review this information and ensure that you understand it and its implications for your documentation work.

Make two copies of all the written information about the system you are documenting. Keep one as a master copy and make notes on the other

EXHIBIT 3-1

Resource Identification Form

Data	Source	Date
Sequential procedures for changing existing records	System specs, run through program screens, screen printouts, verify with PJH (Project Program Dir.)	10/15
Sequential procedures for deleting existing records	System specs, run through program screens, screen printouts, verify with PJH	10/15
Error messages for changes or deletes	Program, verify with PJH	10/15
Commands and keys used for changes or deletes	Technical documentation, program, screens, verify with PJH	10/15
Screens for changes or deletes	Printout from system	10/8

and/or cut and paste it into your source notes. These source notes can be a series of file folders in which you collect information according to the sections of your guide. This is discussed in more detail in the Data Management section of this chapter.

Computer-Generated Information

This type of information consists primarily of reports (output) and copies of data entry and other display screens, such as menus. It also may include copies of the source code. For example, standard Cobol programs contain one section that lists all the error messages. By skimming the program, you can see when these messages are generated. You can also check to see in what circumstances users will receive the messages. Sometimes an error message may be included in a program, but there is nothing that generates it. Documenting this for users would just add confusion.

For many documentation specialists, reading programs is like reading a foreign language. It is not necessary to be a programmer to be a documentation specialist. Far more important is knowledge of the proper use of the English language, knowledge of adult-learning theories, and a creative and logical mind. It is impossible for documentation specialists to be expert in all the programming languages they might work with during their careers. Also, languages are changing. Most are becoming easier to understand. There are rules of logic for each programming language. Nevertheless, there may be more than one way to write the procedures for a particular function.

Approach computer program printouts as one more source of background information—not the only one, and, usually, not the most important. Appendix C on computer languages gives a brief overview of the most common languages. As you would with other research techniques, first define what information you need to get from the program printout. Is this the best source of information? How can it be identified within the program?

Be sure to read the embedded comments within the program. Some programmers are very careful to document their work in this way, and you may gain additional insights into what the program does.

Personal Interviews

Frequently, particularly in the case of new programs or programs under development, interviews will be your primary source of information. Sometimes systems analysts and programmers are reluctant to share system specifications with outsiders, and in most companies, documentation specialists are still considered outsiders, whether they are on staff or contractors.

In the past, programmers were regarded as being somewhat like medieval magicians. No one quite understood how they created their output—it seemed like magic. The industry had few standards, and there was little formal training other than instruction in how to write code. In all fairness, some revisions are necessary whenever a new field is being developed. Trial and error is a legitimate technique in that case. Nevertheless, many programs written on established principles are sloppy at best. The more that outsiders understand the so-called magic, the more responsible and attentive programmers have to be. The result sometimes is unconscious resentment.

If you know your job, are organized and professional in your approach, and have management's support for the idea that you and the programming staff are peers working at different tasks on the same team, you will avoid problems. In many companies, the catch is the last item—management support. You may need to take some time from your regular tasks to put together a presentation about the importance of documentation. Request a meeting with your supervisors, present them with your data, and ask for their *visible* support of your work, including memos and personal conversations with those whom you need to contact for cooperation. Be specific about what you want.

Obtain the bulk of the information you need from established, formal interviews with other people. Do not go into someone's office and ask casually, "What can you tell me about the DCP Accounting package?" Follow these steps:

1 Learn as much as you can about the system from existing documents.

2 Prepare your questions in advance.

3 Determine who has the information you need.

4 Send a memo to those persons requesting a meeting and describing the information you need.

5 Contact them personally after they have received the memo to determine the date and time of the meeting and to reassure them that the process will not be an ordeal.

6 Be punctual and prepared for your interview. Let people know your agenda at the beginning and proceed through your questions. Be sure to ask some open-ended questions to enable respondents to provide information you may not have asked for specifically and to emphasize the points they think are important.

7 Thank them at the end of the interviews and in writing a day or two after the meeting. State that if you have additional questions you would like to call them, and, likewise, if they have additional information that they think would be useful, to please let you know.

8 If appropriate, send a copy of your thank-you memo to the respondents' supervisors.

Some interviewing tips include the following:

1 Arrange a time and place for the interview that is comfortable for both you and the respondent and discourage interruptions.

2 Establish that you and the respondent have a shared goal regarding the interview.

3 Use terminology appropriate to the respondent's work.

4 Keep the need for relevance, validity, and reliability in mind during the interview.

5 Maintain rapport with the respondent.

6 Clearly communicate specific questions in accordance with the purpose of the interview.

7 Detect and correct any misunderstandings the respondent has about the questions.

8 Help the respondent stick to the point.

9 Remember that interviewing is a "spectator sport"—observe the respondent's behavior and guide your own to facilitate the flow of information.

10 Take accurate notes.

Taping this type of interview is rarely useful. The time required to transcribe the tape cuts into the schedule, and often much that is said is irrelevant—yet that gets transcribed too. When you take notes, you know what is important, and that is what gets written down and emphasized. In addition, respondents are often intimidated by tape recorders, and it might create tension and limit the scope of their answers.

There may be times when taping is helpful. For example, it sometimes is difficult to get accurate notes when interviewing over the telephone. Be sure to inform the person you are taping the conversation. Telephone-tape recorder connectors are available for most portable tape recorders and are inexpensive.

DATA MANAGEMENT

The groups of files you will want to maintain include the following:

1 Project management

2 Research

3 First draft

4 Draft with revisions

5 Review copies

6 Final draft

7 Final copy

8 Final-copy graphics and printouts

Establish a specific location, in your desk or a nearby file cabinet, for current project files. If you have more than one project running simultaneously, color code the files by project. You can also color code the groups of files, e.g., project management files might have a red circle on each file tab, and research files might have a green circle on each file tab. Maintaining consistent color-coding practices will save you time when working with data.

Project Management Files

The complexity of the project determines the number of files included in project management. Use your discretion to establish these files in the most useful manner. Information to be included would be the project management plan, schedules, outline for the guide, a program or system profile, correspondence related to the project, time sheets, expense record forms, and other related information.

Research Files

Maintain one file for original source material. Copies of that material and other data should be filed according to the section of the manual to which they refer.

The first rule for the management of research data is similar to the first rule for designing user guides. You must determine how the information is going to be used. Determine the section of the manual to which it refers. Also ask, is it background information or is it data to be incorporated directly into the text?

The research files are vital to the actual writing process. Many documentation specialists do not organize their research materials properly. Few seem to realize that if this step is done correctly, writing the first draft is an easy process. One mistake many people make is to organize data by its source rather than by its subject matter within the context of the finished user guide. For example, suppose you have printouts of a list of error messages for data entry and sample reports. You should not file them together under *Printouts*. Instead, the error message list should go in a file designated *Data Entry,* and the sample reports should go in an *Output* or *Sample Reports* file.

It may seem difficult to organize research material when you have several pages of notes from one interview covering all aspects of the documentation. Planning for this ahead of time will facilitate your note taking during the interview. Leave space between paragraphs; give each paragraph a concise subject head in the margin; underline the key idea in the paragraph if you have time and are sure what it is (otherwise this can be done easily after the interview).

Take time after the interview to categorize by user-guide subjects the topics that the respondent discussed. Make a copy of your notes, and put the original in the original source material file. If it is a particularly large and complex project, you may want this in a separate file labeled with the respondent's name. Cut and paste the copy of your notes into separate subject areas with the date and respondent's initials in the upper right-hand corner of the first page of each section.

Once you know the sections you will have in the guide, set up at least one file for each section. For sections with voluminous notes and several subsections, you may want to add additional files. Label the files *Research* plus the name of the section (and subsection, if appropriate), or use a color-coded label to indicate these are research files. To ensure that you have all the information required, make a list of the necessary data, tape it on the inside cover of each section's file, and check off each item as you add it to the file.

If you follow these steps, you will have all the information you need in one place when you are ready to write a section.

First-Draft File

As you write the first draft, keep it all in one file. Tape an outline of the guide to the inside cover of the file and check off each section after it has been completed. If your first draft is typed or in longhand, you may keep it in this file until it is ready for word processing. If you are working on a large project, you may need one file for your first draft and an additional file for the word processed first draft. Keep this file until the project is completed.

Revised-Draft File

There will be changes after you review, proof, and edit the word-processed draft. Once these corrections have been made on the word-processed copy, keep them in this file. Keep this file at least until the project has been completed.

Review File

After a complete draft has been finished, the review process begins. This may be in-house or client review. In either case, copies of what has been sent for review and the name of the person doing the reviewing, his or her telephone number, and the date the copy is to be returned are kept in this file. The review comments should also be placed here. Keep this file for at least six months after the guide has been released (and longer if space permits) in case any verification is needed.

Final-Draft File

After technical review and other final changes, additional corrections will have to be made. The final-draft file contains the final marked-up copy. It is a good idea to keep this file at least six to eight months after release of the guide.

Final-Copy File and Final-Copy Graphics File

These files are used to protect word-processed or camera-ready copy. Use one file for text and another for graphics and printouts if they require special production procedures. Otherwise, keep the graphics in place in the final copy. Make sure these files are kept in a clean place and receive minimal handling.

FOUR

Creating Written User Guides

"This page has been intentionally left blank."

"You're pretty smart for your age, you got that right."

"Entry of an 'N' . . . Entry of outlet . . . Entry of Full. . . ."

"Allows the user to traverse the network in a user-defined fashion from a particular node in the network."

"The operator can either ⟨cr⟩ to over-ride this field or enter the desired discount price amount."

ORGANIZATION AND ENVIRONMENT

Writers have two major problems—knowing where to start and knowing when to stop. If you effectively organize the information collected before you begin the writing phase, these problems are easily resolved. If you don't, you may end up with a manual that reads like one of the preceding excerpts.

You are involved in a process. It began with the use analysis, which led to user profiles, which served as a basis for defining the project goal, which served to establish the parameters for the preliminary content organization, which led to the project resource parameters and the project management plan. Then the microframe elements were added to produce the writing action plan.

Take out the user profiles, preliminary content organization, and writing action plan. These management tools and what you have learned in your preliminary research will provide a framework for verifying that the content, format, and style you have selected are appropriate. Exhibit 4-1 demonstrates this decision process.

Adjust the content, format, and style to the realities of the situation and define them in more detail. One possibility is to list each section or concept you think belongs in each user guide on an index card or self-stick notepaper. Don't try to put them in any order, just list every possibility, one to a card. Keep in mind the user tasks required by the program; the step-by-step instructions for performing those tasks; and related information, such as system conventions and messages.

Possible components of written user guides include the following:

1 Preface material, including disclaimer and copyright

2 System overview

3 System process diagram

4 Introductory note to reader on how to use the manual

5 Tutorial (a step-by-step instruction method to build confidence and provide users with hands-on experience in performing tasks or functions, e.g., writing a memo in a word processing system or setting up a new personnel record in a payroll system)

6 A section explaining the user interface with the computer hardware

---

EXHIBIT 4-1

Writing Plan Decision Process

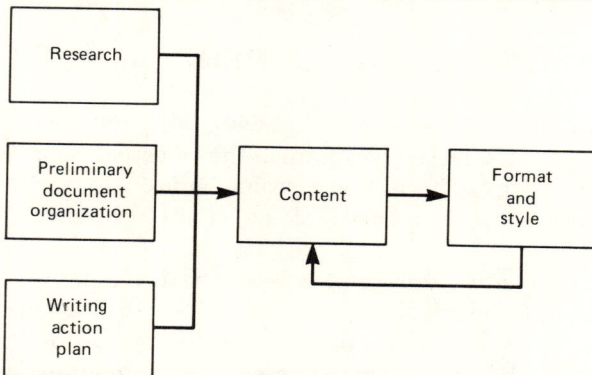

7 List of sequential entry procedures by function

8 List of data maintenance (update) procedures

9 List of output procedures

10 Sample output

11 List of error messages

12 List of commands

13 List of communications protocols

14 Data dictionary

15 Glossary

16 Index

When you have finished, sort through the cards and make a notation using either different colored pens or a symbol on each card to indicate that card's level of importance. Then arrange the cards in logical order. This order should be based on the end users' need for the information. Selection order is based on chronology, importance, use, or difficulty. Decide on format and style considerations for each section and note them for inclusion in your stylebook. You have just created the beginning of your project stylebook and an outline, which can help you with the writing process.

If you are working on a script either for an audio cassette self-paced training program, videotape training program, or other audio-visual format, use the same process for organization but adapt your sections to the particular medium. Less information can be included. See *Script Models: A Handbook for the Media Writer*[1] or another similar script stylebook for guidance.

Posters and three-dimensional desktop aids may be used for specific types of information, e.g., error messages or commands used for data entry. Do not introduce unrelated information on one poster or desktop aid. Here, the assistance of a graphic designer is essential.

There is no single way of organizing information for a particular type of documentation. All user manuals do not have to start with an overview followed by sequential procedures, error messages, and a reference section. Analyzed needs guide the decisions about content. Exhibit 4-2 shows two possible outlines for a text-editing program.

The first outline would be appropriate for a defined end user, e.g., a

[1]Robert Lee and Robert Misiorowski, Hastings House Publishers, New York, 1978.

EXHIBIT 4-2

Sample Outlines

Outline 1

How to Use the Manual
System Overview
Getting Started
Tutorial: Word Processing a Memo
Letters and Memos
Envelopes
Reports
Forms and Contracts
Additional Uses
Glossary
Index

Outline 2

How to Use the Manual
System Overview
Use of the Keyboard (alphabetical by function performed, e.g., center, insert,
    move, with examples)
Cross-reference Table of Functions and Keys
Printing: from the Screen, from Files
Error Messages
Glossary
Index

---

law firm just buying the system. It is designed to familiarize novice users with the system quickly and to enable them to produce legal documents in less than one day. The second outline would be appropriate for an off-the-shelf program that would not be overwhelming in size while still containing all the information to be included.

The outline should be written and refined until it can serve as a trail map for the writing process. The outline is for your use, but it can be sent to a supervisor or to a client if approval is required. The main consideration is to use a numbering and/or lettering system that distinguishes clearly between major and minor sections and subsections.

The sample outlines and many of the comments here are directed toward user guides. Nevertheless, the same organization process applies to other written user aids, such as quick reference cards, training support materials, and audio cassettes.

Where and how you write affects what you write. You need a private office, an answering machine or secretary to take telephone messages, a large desk or working table, shelves and filing drawers for reference and documentation materials, access to a terminal and the programs that are being documented, and whatever else it takes to provide a creative workplace.

Recommended reference books include, at a minimum, *The Elements of Style*;[2] *Roget's International Thesaurus*;[3] *Webster's Third International Dictionary*, unabridged;[4] a small dictionary; a spelling dictionary; a grammar handbook, such as *Hodge's Harbrace College Handbook*;[5] and *The Chicago Manual of Style*.[6] Do not overlook the importance of the environment as a key to an effective work style. Avoid interruptions when you are writing or thinking about what you will be writing. Explain clearly and politely to other staff your closed-door policy.

If you do not have established work patterns, try this method to complete the first draft of each section with breaks only between sections. Start with an easy section and use that as a model for other sections with similar formats. Follow the outline and concentrate on one component at a time. During revisions you can check how it fits into the whole. Here you want to be specific, complete, and narrowly focused. Write only about the subject of the section on which you are working. Do not go back and make corrections until a section is completed. If you have thoughts that go off on a tangent from what you are writing, make notes in the margins or set off the ideas by brackets or asterisks in the text. Do not forget your audience. Keep them in mind as you are writing, and the end result will be a draft that is on target.

CONTENT

The content of user guides comprises instructions, reference data, and system or function descriptions. Accuracy and user comprehension are the hallmarks of documentation content. Accuracy can be ensured through careful research (which is discussed in Chapter 3), the thoughtful selection of words to express concepts and procedures, and an established review process. User comprehension results from using the user profile and other project management tools to guide decisions on specific content.

---

[2]William Strunk, Jr., and E. B. White, Macmillan, New York, 1959.

[3]Crowell, New York, 1946.

[4]Merriam, Springfield, Mass., 1981.

[5]John C. Hodge and Mary E. Whitten, Harcourt, Brace, Jovanovich, New York, 1977.

[6]University of Chicago Press, Chicago, 1982.

There is always the question of what level of detail to include. The point is not to tell everything you know but to provide the user with information to proceed. You can test user comprehension by giving the draft documentation to someone with no knowledge of the system and observing their use of the material. One specific means of enhancing comprehension is to summarize what is about to be learned at the beginning of each section. Exhibit 4-3 shows one form this might take. Here, the Purpose section tells the user what they are about to do in the lesson that follows. This particular example is from a tutorial.

There are five main ways of writing documentation instructions:

1 Cookbook

2 Parallel form or screen

3 Prose

4 Playscript

5 Foundation

Cookbook style starts with an imperative verb—e.g., enter, search, recall—and lists the instructions in sequential order. This style is used frequently for tutorials and data entry, data maintenance, and data output procedures. See Exhibit 4-4 for two examples. Each instruction may

---

EXHIBIT 4-3

Sample Synopsis Preceding Instructions

PURPOSE: The DIRECTORY command is used to display a list of all the current subsets of a particular database. Here, you will examine the Test Database subsets. The subsets will be listed, with the number of items in each subset, the date the subset was created, the date it was last modified, and the keyword used for access to the subset.

LESSON:

1. Enter *DIR.TEST* or *DIRECTORY.TEST*
2. The Test Database will be displayed on the screen
3. Identify the keyword for the Solar Office dataset
4. Enter the keyword for the Solar Office dataset
5. The Master Menu for the Solar Office dataset will be displayed
6. Enter *5* to return to the Test Database Master Menu and the next command exercise

EXHIBIT 4-4

Sample Cookbook-Style Instructions

---

1. Enter **1** if the Product Type is Agricultural; Enter **2** if the Product Type is Consumer
   Field size = 1
   Note: This is a key data field that is required; if you do not enter a number, the system will default to 1

2. Enter the Machine Serial Number
   Field Size = 8
   Note: This is a key data field that is required; if you do not enter a number, the system will default to 0

3. Enter the List Price with the decimal
   Field Size: 11; Numeric
   Sample: **34369.** is $34,369.00

4. Enter the Date Acquired in MMDDYY format
   Field Size: 6; Numeric
   Sample: **091581** is September 15, 1981

Example 1

Enter your name followed immediately by . with no space
Press RETURN to move cursor to next line
Enter your password
   [NOTE: if you do not have a password, see the data processing manager to obtain one]
Press RETURN immediately after your password
Enter the date in MMDDYY format

Example 2

---

be written as a sentence or a phrase and may be numbered or not. These considerations are discussed in the following section on format and style.

There is variation in the style conventions used in this book for data entry instructions. The purpose of the variation is to provide some examples of the different options for instructions. An example of one set of conventions is as follows:

1 Keys are capitalized, e.g., press RETURN.

2 Names of display screens and menus in the text have the first letter capitalized, e.g., the Tenant Record Data Entry Screen, the Tenant Rent Records Menu.

3   Names of screens and menus in a screen exhibit are presented as they appear on the actual screen.

4   All data, punctuation, and blank spaces entered by the user are underlined.

    a.   Specified data to be typed is printed in bold and capitalized, e.g., enter **HELP**

    b.   Unspecified data are in parentheses, e.g., enter (your name)

To define the conventions for a specific project, review the research material and make a list of all the elements that need to be presented. This list might include: keys, menus, display screens, data entry screens, user-entered data, error messages, systems prompts, and command names. Be sure to define the manual conventions at the beginning of the manual.

Guidelines for developing conventions include the following:

1   Use a different style for each type of information unless types can be grouped together logically.

2   Present information displayed on the screen in a form as close as possible to the displayed version.

3   Ensure that user-entered information is clear and that punctuation is not included unless it is part of the data to be entered.

4   Identify screen representations by *reversal* (the background is dark and the print is white), boxing, or other appropriate graphic delineation; ensure that screen representations are titled correctly, are legible, and represent exactly what the user will see.

5   Ensure that your conventions do not conflict with the form in which information is presented to the user throughout the system.

Parallel, or *screen form,* lists instructions according to numbers on a form, such as a data entry form, or line numbers on a display screen. It is usually used for data entry. The numbers of the instructions must coincide with the numbers on the form or screen. See Exhibit 4-5 for an example of this style used in a data entry procedure for a personnel record.

Prose style explains a procedure in paragraph format using complete sentences. Notes and explanations may be included as shown in Exhibit 4-6.

Playscript style is used when more than one person is involved in data manipulation. The job title is listed in the left-hand margin with the

EXHIBIT 4-5

Sample Parallel or Screen Form Instructions

NEW PERSONNEL RECORD FORM

(1)NAME:
(2)ADDRESS:
(3)″
(4)″
(5)SOCIAL SECURITY #:
(6)START DATE OF EMPLOYMENT:
(7)JOB TITLE:

Manual Instructions

NEW PERSONNEL RECORD FORM LINE NUMBER	DATA PROCESSING ENTRY
(1)	Enter the name of the new employee on line 1 of the screen, last name first, up to 80 characters; if the name is longer than 80 characters, abbreviate the first name or use an initial for the first name. Press **RETURN** after the last character entered.
(2) through (4)	Enter the street address or post office box on line 2; the city, state (using U.S. Postal Service two-character abbreviations) and zip code on line 3. If the address is unusually long, line 4 may be used, but keep each line as it should appear on a mailing label; up to 80 characters per line are allowed. Press **RETURN** after the last character entered on each line of the screen. NOTE: Access Help Screen 3 if you do not know the state two-character abbreviations by entering **HELP.3**; return to the screen you were working on by entering **SCREEN.2.**
(5)	Enter the new employee's Social Security number on the next empty line, which is marked (5) on the sample form but may be line 4 or 5 on the screen, depending on how many lines were used for the address. Press **RETURN** after the last character entered.
(6)	Enter the start date of employment on the next line in MMDDYY format [EXAMPLE: July 6, 1985, is entered 070685]. Press **RETURN** after the last character entered.
(7)	Enter the job description, which may be up to 80 characters. Enter **FILE.2** after the last character entered to create a file of this data. The screen will be cleared. If you do not wish to create a file and want to correct an entry in this record, press **RETURN** and the cursor will move to the first line. If you wish to return to the Data Entry Menu, enter **MENU.1.**

Sample Prose-Style Instructions

OFFSET: The offset is the top margin of a page. It is the number of lines from the top of the paper to the first line of text. It is measured in terms of lines; there are six (6) lines to an inch. To set the offset for a new document, press CMD and enter the letter **O** followed by the number of lines you select for the offset, then press RETURN. For example, to set an offset of 1½ inches, you would press CMD, then enter **O9.**

instructions on the right side. The instructions are numbered sequentially and do not start again with number 1 at the beginning of each section in which a new person is introduced. Exhibit 4-7 is an example of play-script-style instructions for an inventory control system.

Foundation style is used for flexible systems in which the end user can customize the programs and for which there are no set input procedures that produce established output. Certain functions of database management systems are one example of this type of program. It is expected that this is one area in which applications software will be expanding in the next few years. Foundation style can be divided into five components:

1 Explanations of what users can do with the program and why they might be using it, i.e., the raison d'être of the program

2 Implications, effects, and possible outputs of the program

3 Generic steps to be followed

4 Examples of different types of uses

5 Reference data, including constraints such as field length, and possible errors

Reference data is presented most frequently in tables or lists. Take care to include all the necessary information. For example, in an error message table include the message as the user receives it, an explanation of how to correct it, and an example of the corrected form. Also, organize the reference data in a logical sequence, usually alphabetically. Reference data might include error messages, a data dictionary, or a list of commands. A sample data dictionary is shown in Exhibit 4-8. Other columns that might be included are abbreviations if the field name is abbreviated, the source of the data, and the range for numeric data, e.g., DD (day) would be 01 through 31. The data dictionary also could be organized by

EXHIBIT 4-7

Sample Playscript-Style Instructions

Personnel	Procedures
Order clerk	When order is made: 1 Enter order data on Screen 1 according to screen prompts 2 To open this order as a record under supplier, move cursor to highlight supplier number you entered on this screen and press **RETURN**
Data processing clerk	When invoice is received: 3 To recall supplier, enter supplier number and press **RECALL** 4 Press **SEARCH,** enter invoice number, press **RETURN** Cursor moves to invoice item 5 Press **CLEAR** to remove other information from the screen 6 Enter **INVENTORY ITEM** on line 1 of the screen, press **RETURN** to update this item to the Inventory Control File
Inventory control clerk	When item is used: 7 Enter **ITEM CODE NUMBER** where it is called for on Screen 5, press **RETURN** to update the record [NOTE: if you are unsure of Item Code Number but you know the Item Name, recall Screen 20 by entering **HELP 20** and locating the item, which is listed alphabetically; if you know the Item Serial Number, recall Help Screen 25 by entering **HELP 25** and locating the serial number, which is listed numerically in ascending order; the Item Code Number is cross-referenced on both Help Screens 20 and 25]

the English version of the field name if that is how the end user would look it up.

This type of reference information lends itself to quick reference cards and posters as a memory refresher for infrequent users or infrequently used functions of the system. The graphic display of reference data is an important consideration for ease of use. Chapter 6 contains additional information on graphic presentations.

System or function descriptions usually combine a text writing style

EXHIBIT 4-8

Data Dictionary

Field Name	Description	Alphanumeric/ Numeric	Print Length	Sample Field Value
ALPHASORT	Manufacturer name used for alphabetical sorting	A	25 variable	DCP MANUFACTURING
STATE	Manufacturer state	A	2 fixed	CO
UNITDIM	Unit dimensions	N	6 variable	6.58 3.18 4.63
UNITWT	Weight of unit in pounds	N	6 fixed	120
TELNO	Manufacturer telephone number	N	12 fixed	303/555-1212

and appropriate graphics. Such descriptions may be used in a system overview and summaries of each section. The final draft of the system overview or introduction should be written last, after you have thoroughly familiarized yourself with the system, although it may be helpful to write a rough draft of the overview first to give yourself a framework for understanding the program.

STYLE

"Proper words in proper places," wrote Jonathan Swift in 1720. A few years later the Earl of Chesterfield told his son that "style is the dress of thoughts." There are two concepts of style important to the technical writer: the mode and form of communication separate from its content; and a particular style that can be attributed to a person, period, or other identifiable group, such as the Impressionist style of painting, the literary style of Chaucer, journalistic style, or the DHH Software Systems documentation style.

   Style plus content equals meaning. A good way to develop a sense of style is to read good writing and "listen" to it, that is, pay attention to the use, pattern, and rhythm of the words. *The Wall Street Journal* and *The New York Times* provide some of the best journalistic writing in the United States. It is more difficult to find good examples of technical writing. Compare the following two product descriptions:

1 The DMO Module plugs directly into the digital I/O slot of the Model 43. It can be used with most computers which have a 16-bit parallel I/O capability. All signals are TTL compatible, and either "ground-true" or "positive-true" logic can be accommodated.

2 The DCP Model is a *speaker-dependent recognition system* that recognizes individual words and phrases. It operates by comparing the spoken word to a vocabulary previously entered by the user.

Neither of these examples demonstrates outstanding writing style, but the latter gives the reader less jargon and explains the so-called speaker-dependent recognition system. In both cases, model identification has been changed to protect the guilty.

   Examining words, sentences, and paragraphs to ensure their clarity of meaning is the first step toward good style. Other helpful techniques include the following:

1 Being consistent in punctuation, word use, and format conventions

2 Using a cut-and-paste technique or the word processing equivalent to move words, phrases, sentences, and paragraphs around so that they clearly build to a point

3 Putting aside written work for a day or two before reviewing it

4 Disciplining yourself to cut out excess words even if they sound good

5 Using resources such as dictionaries, a thesaurus, grammar handbooks, and several stylebooks

6 Understanding your needs for a productive writing environment

7 Knowing your work pace

The second concept of style—a particular style attributable to an identifiable group—is the motivation for developing your own stylebook, for defining specifically the conventions to be used by a company or for a particular document. Here, "consistency" is the key word.

Words

As the artist has color, the author has words. Think of the palette available. Select with care and knowledge of meaning. Remember the following: Avoid jargon, beware of ambiguity in meaning, and be conscious of the context in which you use words with two or more meanings. Precise word use is essential in technical writing, and that applies to all words, not just technical terms. Technical writing requires conciseness as well as preciseness. Exhibit 4-9 lists several misused words and their correct meaning and use. Exhibit 4-10 provides a list of unnecessarily wordy or pretentious phrases and their more concise synonyms.

Words that describe a broad category should not be used if the specific is meant. For example, change "computer technology is affecting family relationships" to "microcomputers are affecting family relationships" if that is exactly what is meant.

Avoiding "Computerese." Computer industry jargon is the most common problem in user guides. It is difficult to insist on the accurate use of English when everyone around you speaks computerese and there is a certain amount of status in understanding the cryptic acronyms or imprecise phrases that "everybody" knows. Nevertheless, it is your responsibility as a communicator to fight for accurate, precise language. Jargon does not provide that. Consider the following example, which is a definition:

XXX: The screen on which the application should define its windows.

EXHIBIT 4-9

Word Selection and Use

Affect: influence; see "effect." Good documentation can affect the efficiency of the data entry operator.

All ready: prepared; see "already." Everything is all ready for the first test program.

Already: previously; see "all ready." This batch has been run already.

Among: in the midst of, in connection with; see "between." One chooses among several objects.

Amount: aggregate; see "number." Writing a program is a great amount of work.

Between: involving, connecting; see "among." One selects between two objects. Note that "between" may be used for more than two objects if they are directly related, e.g., This system can communicate between four computers.

Bi: every two; see "semi." The user newsletter is published bimonthly (every two months).

Bisect: cut in two. A line cannot bisect a terminal screen.

Can: am (is, are) able; see "may." She can program in Basic, but she may not use my personal computer to do so.

Compare to: list similarities of different types of things. Writing documentation can be compared to skydiving.

Compare with: list differences between objects in the same category. The Apple II may be compared with the IBM Personal Computer.

Comprise: include. The manual comprises the following sections: Introduction, Input, System Control, Output, References.

Continual: over and over again, repeated; see "continuous." This microcomputer has been used continually.

Continuous: unbroken, uninterrupted; see "continual." A sine wave is a continuous pattern.

Effect: (v.) accomplish; see "affect." The technical writer effected a change in the documentation style.

Either: refers to one or the other of two; see "neither"; is singular. Either the DCP word processing program or the DXD text-editing program is available.

Ensure: to make an outcome inevitable, secure; see "insure." Ensure that this program is debugged before it is released.

Fewer: refers to number; see "less." There are fewer prompts in the new program.

Farther: expressing physical distance; see "further." The hotel is farther than I thought.

Further: expresses additional degree or quantity; see "farther." The DMO microcomputer is further advanced than this brand.

However: at the beginning of a sentence, means in whatever way or to whatever extent; see "nevertheless." However you complete this manual, it will be an improvement.

Exhibit 4-9, *Continued*

Word Selection and Use

Insure: refers to insurance for people or objects; see "ensure." The company insures its employees.

Less: refers to degree or value; see "fewer." The new program takes less time to run.

May: possibility, permission; see "can." You may leave at 5:00 p.m.

Neither: refers to one or the other of two; see "either"; is singular. Neither of these programs works.

Nevertheless: in spite of that, yet; see "however." Tutorials are overused; nevertheless, they can serve a purpose in certain user manuals.

Number: sum of separate units; see "amount." This project involves a large number of tasks.

Percent: by the hundred, used to express proportions or rates; see "percentage points." Sales of the DXD software program have increased from 10 percent of the total market share to 20 percent, which is an increase of 100 percent.

Percentage points: specific units of percent; see "percent." Sales of the DXD software program have increased from 10 percent of the total market share to 20 percent, which is an increase of 10 percentage points.

Persons: refers to an exact or small number; see "people." There are five persons in the waiting room.

People: refers to a large number; see "persons." Many people have home computers.

Semi: half; see "bi." The manual is updated semiannually (twice a year).

That: a pronoun used to introduce restrictive clauses; see "which." Look at the software program that is on the microcomputer now.

When: at a specific moment; see "while." The programmer may leave when the computer is turned off.

Which: a pronoun used to introduce nonrestrictive clauses; usually preceded by a comma; see "that." The DXD software program, which was designed in-house, is a database management system.

While: during the time that; see "when." The programmer must be present while the program is running.

What do you think that means? Actually it means the following:

XXX: The screen on which this routine defines the prototype windows to be used in the application program.

The argument given in support of the first definition was that this system is for programmers and they will understand. Nonsense. Imprecise language in the first example lead to a statement that is not accurate.

EXHIBIT 4-10

Word Substitutions

Change	To	Change	To
Accordingly	So	In addition to	Also
Accounted for by the fact that	Because	Inasmuch as	Because
Activate	Start	In order to	To
Additional	Extra, more	Insofar as	If
After the conclusion of	After	In the event that	If
Aggregate	Total, sum	Is applicable	Applies
A great deal of	Much	Is defined as	Is
A number of	Many, several	Is dependent upon	Depends on
Along the lines	Like, similar to	Is equipped with	Has
As a whole	Entire	Is similar to	Like, resembles
As far as ... is concerned	This	Maximal	Highest, most
As long as	Because	Necessitate	Require
At all times	Always	One of the reasons	A reason, one reason
At the present time	Now	Prior to	Before
Based on the fact that	Because	Subsequently	After, later
Commence	Begin	Subsequent to	After
Due to the fact that	Because	The foregoing	These, those
During the time that	While	The question as to whether	Whether
Evident	Clear, plain	This is a subject that	This
Finalize	Complete, conclude	Through the use of	By, which
For the purpose of	For, to	With reference to	About, concerning
Give consideration to	Consider	With regard to	About, concerning
If and when	If	With the exception of	Except
In accordance with	By, from	With the result that	Resulted

To avoid imprecise instructions, make sure you understand exactly what is to be done, then write it in your own words. From that draft, you can build an accurate, precise statement.

Should you use "type" or "enter"; should you write "the screen asks" or "the screen displays"? Correct terminology is another way of using precise language. "Enter" and "type" mean two different things. "Enter" implies two actions, typing on the keyboard and pressing an ENTER or RETURN key to actually enter the data. If you are describing that combination of actions as one (and you have explained that), use "enter." "Ask" and "display" also are different, but not necessarily mutually exclusive. Is the emphasis on requiring a response? If so, "ask" is more appropriate.

This brings up another point. Does "ask" anthropomorphize the computer? Grammarians may argue that it does. It is a borderline term, but a phrase such as "the computer doesn't like it when you hit the wrong key" is not only trite but clearly anthropomorphic. Computers do not have the capability to like or not like anything. Do not endow your computers with human characteristics.

You can enhance a user's understanding of any system by using accurate, precise terms and avoiding jargon. In this way, you will not fall victim to "computerese: a terminal disease."

Acronyms and Abbreviations.   Use acronyms with care and identify the complete words first, e.g., *random access memory* (RAM). In additional references, RAM can be used alone. Appendix B contains a list of common computer and electronics acronyms and abbreviations.

Sexism.   Language is a reflection of behavior and values; ensure that your language reflects no bias on the basis of sex. Using "he" as the unknown antecedent is sexist, as are the terms "chairman," "salesman," "female computer programmer," "man's achievements," and similar expressions. There are alternatives. For example, the sentence can be rewritten in the plural, the pronoun dropped, nonsexist words substituted for sexist ones, "s/he" or "she/he" written in place of "he." Samples of nonsexist word substitutions include "businessperson," "business owner," or "business executive" for "businessman"; "council member" for "councilman"; "synthetic" or "manufactured" for "man-made"; "coordinator," "moderator," or "chair" for "chairman"; "people," "humanity," or "human beings" for "mankind."

Examples of sentence changes are: ""The user enters **D** to delete the line; he enters **C** to change the format" can be changed to "To delete a line, enter **D**. To change the format, enter **C**." "Give each salesman a copy of the documentation for his subject area" can be changed to "Give the sales staff copies of the documentation for their particular areas." "The average technical writer has two persons on his staff" can be changed to "The average technical writer has two staff persons" or "The average technical writer has two persons on her or his (or her/his) staff."

Hyphenated Words. To hyphenate or not to hyphenate seems to be one of the biggest word problems facing writers. There are rules that govern hyphenation, and when in doubt, there is *Webster's Third New International Dictionary* (unabridged).

Prefixes and Suffixes. Words with prefixes and suffixes generally are not hyphenated. There are a few exceptions, but the rules can be learned quickly. Prefixed words in which the meaning could be confused are hyphenated. Examples include "re-create" (meaning to create anew), "re-cover" (meaning to cover again), and "re-search" (meaning to search again). Words using "self" (except for "selfdom," "selfhood," and "selfless"); and "ex" if it means former and is connected to a noun ("ex-secretary of defense") are hyphenated. If the prefix or suffix causes the same letter to be repeated three times, it is hyphenated, e.g., "bell-like." Words with longer prefixes such as "anti" and "semi" are hyphenated if the final vowel of the prefix is doubled, e.g., "anti-intellectual," "semi-infinite." "Microorganism" is an exception. Words with "non" as a prefix are not hyphenated, but beware of Latin phrases in which "non" is a word such as "non sequitur" or "non possums." If the prefix is duplicated in the word, a hyphen is used, e.g., "re-redirect." Words with a prefix followed by a capitalized word always are hyphenated, e.g., "inter-American," and "pre-Columbian."

Compound Words and Modifiers. Words made up of two or more words or with more than one modifier are hyphenated to avoid confusion. Note the difference between "small-business owner" and "small business-owner." The former is an owner of a small business; the latter, a small person who owns a business. Phrases such as "step-by-step procedures" and "off-the-shelf programs" are hyphenated because the hyphenated words express a single thought and modify another word. Compound modifiers that precede the modified word are hyphenated if they help to clarify the meaning. A hyphen is not required when you are writing for a knowledgeable target audience, e.g., "database management system" is understood in the industry as a single unit and does not need a hyphen.

Compound Numbers. Compound numbers from twenty-one through ninety-nine and fractions such as one-half are hyphenated unless the fraction is used as a noun, e.g., "Three quarters of the programmers use

Cobol." Numbers used as compound modifiers are hyphenated, e.g., "12-inch screen."

Idiomatic Prepositions.   Many writers use incorrect prepositions in idiomatic phrases. Examples of correct forms include "different from" (not "than"); "independent of" (not "from"); "in search of" (not "for"); and "on a list" (not "in").

Sentences

If words represent the colors of the palette available to the writer, sentences are the lines that create shapes in a composition. If one line is off, the total painting is affected. Sentences need to be both clear and concise. The writer starts with the appropriate words and assembles them to build a specific meaning. Observe the basic rules of grammar, and use a stylebook or grammar handbook if you are unsure of correct use. Some of the more common mistakes in sentence structure are discussed in this section.

Compound Verbs.   Verbs of two or more words are called *compound verbs.* Usually, they should not be separated by inserting adverbs or other words. "The message is given sometimes" should not be written "The message is sometimes given." The compound verb is "is given." Infinitives are a form of compound verb. Occasionally it makes more sense to split an infinitive with its modifier. Use and word emphasis are guides to the writer. For example, "To write effectively is an important goal" is better than "To effectively write is an important goal." Nevertheless, "To effectively write concise documentation is an essential skill" is better than "To write effectively concise documentation is an essential skill." In the latter example, it is unclear whether "effectively" modifies "to write" or "concise."

Location of Modifiers.   Modifiers, whether words, phrases, or clauses, should be placed as close as possible to the word that they are modifying. "Trade journals carried articles about the computer company's success in every part of the country." Does this sentence mean the computer company was successful in every part of the country or that the articles were carried in every part of the country? The sentence is correct if it is to mean the former. To reword the sentence for the latter meaning, write "Trade journals carried articles in every part of the country about the computer company's success."

Dangling Participles.   Participial phrases that do not modify the subject are called *dangling participles.* Look at the sentence, "The first day on the job passed quickly, reviewing old documentation, making notes for new standards, and meeting programmers." Clearly the "day" did not review documentation, make notes, or meet programmers. Rewrite this sentence as, "I quickly passed my first day on the job, reviewing old documentation, making notes for new standards, and meeting programmers."

Agreement of Subject and Verb. Technical writers certainly know that subjects and verbs must agree, but sometimes there is a problem in determining what is the subject. Identify the subject in the following sentences. "Either of these computers may be used." The subject is "either," which is singular, not "computers," which is plural. "Both of these computers work." The subject is "both," which is plural. "The number of programs being developed is large." The subject is "number," which is singular. "The systems analyst, as well as all the programmers, believes the tests can be completed tomorrow." The subject is "systems analyst," which is singular.

If the additional items that add to the subject are listed in a phrase starting with "along with," "as well as," "in addition to," "including," "no less than," "together with," or "with," the verb agrees with the initial subject, which is "systems analyst" in the latter example. "The systems analyst and the chief programmer believe . . . " has a compound subject (the "systems analyst" and the "chief programmer"), which is plural.

Sentence Length. Counting the number of words or syllables in a sentence is an artificial method of determining sentence length. The length is determined by the message to be conveyed and the proper selection and placement of words. To maintain reader interest, sentence lengths should be varied. This can be accomplished without loss of clarity. Read your writing out loud, and you will learn to adjust your work to the rhythm of good writing.

Paragraphs

A paragraph is the main unit of expository writing. It must convey a unified thought. Although good sentences spring from good word choice, it is not true that good paragraphs automatically grow from good sentences. It is essential that you have a clear view of the purpose and direction of the entire document in order to create good paragraphs. Use an outline, an extended table of contents, or any other tool that depicts the purpose and direction of the document section by section.

You should be able to describe the point of each paragraph in a sentence or phrase. Be sure that each sentence relates to this theme. Ensure that the subject of the paragraph does not wander.

There are several patterns in which sentences can be arranged in a paragraph. For example, the topic sentence can be placed first, which is true in this paragraph. This is not a requirement and is determined by the author's overall goals. Other arrangements include chronological, procedural, spatial, order of climax (in which the least important idea is first and the key sentence is placed last), movement from the general to the specific or vice versa.

Like sentences, paragraphs need a transition from one to another. A previously mentioned idea or concept can be repeated and discussed, using a different example or one item in a list that can be discussed in more detail. For example, if the paragraph starts out, "The most commonly used programming languages are Basic, Cobol, Fortran, and Pascal . . . ," the second paragraph might begin by stating, "Basic, a key programming language, is used primarily for home computers and simple business programs. . . ." Other paragraph transition techniques include taking the last thought expressed in one paragraph and describing it in detail in the next, repeating keywords, or starting paragraphs with the same sentence type and style.

Punctuation

Punctuation provides the frame for the canvas. You do not use a round frame for a square painting unless you know exactly the effect you want to create, are aware that you are breaking the rules, and know why you are doing so. Technical writing, particularly documentation, has no business in the realm of aesthetic experimentation. Creativity is required, but not in the use of the English language. A grammar handbook and stylebook along with your dictionary and thesaurus should be within reach when you are writing.

The description of sequential procedures lends itself to a numbered list of steps. Here you can exhibit a modicum of creativity. Full sentences are not required; phrases may be used, and certain items may be in boldface, boxed, or set off by other techniques. The requirements for this type of presentation are: consistency, equal treatment of equal concepts, logical order, and clarity of expression. Exhibits 4-11 and 4-12 show the same sequential procedures presented in two different styles. Note the use of punctuation in each example.

The comma is a form of punctuation much abused by technical writers. The most common error is to leave out the comma after the next to last item in a list of three or more things. Examples of correct use are: "The Apple II, the IBM PC, and the Commodore . . . " or "Information input,

EXHIBIT 4-11

Sample Sequential Procedures—Phrases

---

1. **CONTROL CODE**

   ENTER **AC.**

   AC is the Control Code for the Account Control File; required for access to this file.

2. **BATCH NUMBER**

   ENTER a three-digit **BATCH NUMBER.**

   The Batch Number is required by this company for control purposes; not a system requirement; should be entered on keypunch form, if not, obtain from data processing manager.

3. **ACCOUNT NUMBER**

   ENTER a six-digit **ACCOUNT NUMBER.**

   The Account Number is required by the system for access to this file; for established accounts, it should be entered on the keypunch form, if not, ENTER **SEARCH** and the Account Name or Account Number listed on the keypunch form and key information for this account will be displayed; for new accounts it should be entered on the keypunch form, if not, ENTER **SC** for access to System Control File, then ENTER **NEWNUMBER,** and the next Account Number to be used will be displayed.

---

database management, system control, and information output. . . ." This rule does not apply to journalism or informal writing, but it is applicable to all forms of technical writing. If items in a list are described by non-restrictive clauses set off by commas, the items are separated by a semicolon. For example, "The Apple II, which I use at home; the IBM PC, which my company has bought; and the Commodore, which the university has installed in my computer lab. . . ."

Punctuation inside or outside of quotation marks is another area in which writers frequently err. The period and comma are placed inside quotation marks; the semicolon and colon are placed outside quotation marks; the dash, question mark, and exclamation point are placed inside quotation marks if they apply only to the information enclosed by the quotation marks; otherwise, they are placed outside. Look at the following two examples: "This microcomputer is the 'apple of my eye.'" "This microcomputer is the 'apple of my eye'; it even tells me how to punctuate."

EXHIBIT 4-12

Sample Sequential Procedures—Sentences

1. **CONTROL CODE**

   Enter **AC,** which is the Control Code for the Account Control File, and is required for access to this file.

   > SYSTEM ACCESS REQUIREMENT

2. **BATCH NUMBER**

   Enter a three-digit Batch Number, which is required by this company for control purposes. It is not a system requirement.

   The Batch Number should be entered on the keypunch form. If it is missing, obtain the correct number from the data processing manager.

   > COMPANY REQUIREMENT

3. **ACCOUNT NUMBER**

   Enter a six-digit Account Number, which is required by the system for access to this file and is used by the System Control File.

   For established accounts, the number should be located on the keypunch form. If it is missing, enter **SEARCH** followed by the Account Name *or* the Account Code Number listed on the keypunch form. Key information for this account, including the Account Number, will be displayed on the screen.

   For new accounts, the number also should be located on the keypunch form. If it is missing, enter **SC** for access to the System Control File, then enter **NEWNUMBER.** The next Account Number to be used will be displayed on the screen.

   > SYSTEM CONTROL REQUIREMENT

   > SYSTEM ACCESS REQUIREMENT

These errors are only the most common; there is an almost infinite range of mistakes a writer can make. You are referred again (and again) to a grammar handbook and your own stylebook.

FORMAT

Format is the skeleton of a written document, whereas style breathes life into it. Format covers items such as type style and size, size of paper, margins, spacing, and indentions.

Writers think of a printed page in terms of the information it contains and the means by which it is presented—content and style. Production designers see a printed page in terms of the relationship between the printed matter and white space. That relationship is the key to understanding format. To produce quality software user guides requires as much concern for format as for content and style.

There is an established psychology of how people learn. The manner in which the material is presented strongly affects the learners' perceptions and retention of the information. Accuracy and consistency are not enough. Each printed page must invite the reader to partake, just as a well-set table prompts a diner to sit down.

Spacing is the major consideration in format decisions. Spacing includes space between characters, words, lines of type, paragraphs, and the top, bottom, and side margins of the page. Use conventional spacing and ensure that it is standard throughout the document.

Spacing between paragraphs is usually 50 percent more than spacing between lines. Page image area must be standard throughout a document, with at least a 1-inch border on each of the four sides, and $1\frac{1}{2}$ inches for the left margin if the manual will be bound in a three-ring binder, spiral binder, or other system that takes up space. Set up the margins so that the printed information appears centered on the page after binding. Set standard spacing conventions for the various components—e.g., cookbook-style instructions, reports, and tables—and use them consistently throughout the document. Insufficient white space makes a document look cluttered; too much white space makes it appear incoherent. Seek the advice of professional production designers if you are unsure of what works.

Type is measured in points. One point is 1/72 inch. Most text copy is set in 8- to 12-point type. The lower the number, the smaller the type. Use one type size for the standard document with changes for headings. Tables, figures, and diagrams may be in a size smaller than the text type, but should be compatible with the text.

Headings and subheadings draw attention to important points, let readers find their place in the document, assist readers in locating information quickly, and serve to lead readers through the document. Choose heading titles carefully. Use words and not numbers alone, and ensure that equal weight is given for equal value. Position, type size, and uppercase and lowercase letters are used to differentiate among heading ranks. In terms of ranking, vertically centered headings are superior to flush-left headings, all uppercase is superior to uppercase and lowercase, and, of course, larger type size is superior to smaller type size. Note that titles of ten or more words are difficult to read in all uppercase. Names of lists are not part of the heading hierarchy and can be centered over the list. One very effective means of presenting headings is to create a wide column on the left side of the page.

The use of numbered paragraphs should be avoided because they give the documentation a heavy, overly technical feeling and because each number is just one more item readers have to wade through to get to the valuable information. The only instance in which numbered paragraphs should be used for user guides is when there is extensive cross-referencing and that is the only way readers can find their way around.

Pagination is best within sections, e.g., page 3 of Section 2 Data Entry Procedures would be numbered 3-2 or 3.2. A header or footer could be used with the name of the section, e.g., "Data Entry Procedures" on the inside and the page number on the outside. If both headers and footers are used, there is less room for text. One or the other is usually sufficient. Front matter, such as a preface and disclaimer, is numbered in lowercase Roman numerals, e.g., i, ii.

The most common paper size is $8\frac{1}{2}$ by 11 inches. In a three-ring binder, a guide this size may be difficult to manipulate when sitting at a terminal in a crowded data processing room. On the other hand, it is easier to see text on this page size if it is in a type of easel binder. Using a smaller, nonstandard paper size probably will increase the cost of production and definitely will increase the bulk of the manual. Investigate the implications of using different paper sizes before you make a final decision. Be sure you know the environment in which the manual will be used.

The format decisions belong in the project stylebook so that consistency can be ensured. Also, review the decisions with clerical support staff and production staff to ensure that your decisions fit the options available to you.

CREATING A STYLEBOOK

The Elements of Style by William Strunk, Jr., and E. B. White is one of the best-known stylebooks. A mere 71 pages, it contains a great deal of useful information. Another popular stylebook is the University of Chicago's *The Chicago Manual of Style*. Stylebooks belong next to your grammar handbook. Unfortunately, there is no specific stylebook for technical writing; therefore, you have to create your own. Your stylebook may be for an entire company, the documents produced by your office or department, or for a one-time project.

As with a documentation manual, the audience for a stylebook must be analyzed first. Is it only for you? Is there any possibility others will use it? Is the same document going to be used by writers, editors, and secretaries? Are there clients involved, and do they have to approve it? For how many projects will it be used?

The answers to these questions will determine the formality of the stylebook. Even if it is only for your use, it is best to have it typed on a word processor or text-editing program and to have the printed copy enclosed in a three-ring binder with tabs for each section. Your needs and the project's needs govern the content and categories.

Consider using main headings for text, graphics, format requirements, editing and review procedures and guidelines, production requirements, appendixes, and an index.

Subcategories under text might include the following:

1 Words, including spelling, compound forms, hyphenation, meaning, abbreviations, numbers, and words or expressions to avoid

2 Grammar, which might cover punctuation (further subdivided by each punctuation mark), sentence structure, subject-verb agreement, verb forms, and modifiers

3 Signs and symbols

4 Standard phrases, such as the disclaimer and universal data entry procedures for the systems you are documenting

5 Composition guidelines, such as good writing tips gleaned from various sources

Graphics would include the conventions for presenting various types of graphics, such as display screens, tables, figures, forms, and process diagrams. In addition to itemizing the conventions, include an example of each type. The forms subsection would include the forms created for the writing action plan as well as any forms developed for the documentation manual itself.

Format requirements would vary depending on the document(s) covered, but might include the following:

1 Title page

2 Preface material

3 Margins, tabs, and offset

4 Pagination, including headers, footers, and page numbers

5 Headings and subheadings

6 References

7 Sequential procedures, such as input requirements

8 Screens

9 Output description

Editing and review procedures would include standard editing and proofreading symbols and sample memos and sign-off letters for the review process.

You may not be responsible for production. Nevertheless, it is important to be aware of production requirements. It can save your company money and time. Determine the various production methods that might be used. Interview the persons responsible for production to collect information, outline the procedures, and list any requirements and suggestions they have for preparing final copy. Learn about new developments in production methods, e.g., communication between word processors and typesetting equipment, which eliminates proofing of galley sheets. Include in your stylebook notes on types of production methods and the deliverable requirements for each type. Chapter 8 discusses production methods.

The stylebook appendixes may be used for a glossary, additional reference material, or related articles. An index is invaluable in a document that will be used as frequently as you will use your stylebook. If you do not have time to develop a complete index, write a detailed table of contents with clearly identifiable subheadings.

Chapter

FIVE

Creating On-Line Interactive User Guides

On-line interactive documentation is data accessed on a computer system that helps end users utilize software programs correctly. It also may be called "electronic documentation," "embedded documentation," or "electronic user guides." The importance of this type of documentation will increase, and hard-copy documentation gradually will assume the role of supplemental information, such as initial access instructions and quick reference material. The advantages of on-line interactive documentation are that it is available where and when users need it (it can not be lost or left in the car), it is related directly to the context in which users are working, and it can be kept current with the program more easily than other forms of documentation.

Information that should not be put on-line includes log-on procedures, installation instructions, and what to do if the system crashes. Clearly this is information that can not be accessed when it is needed if it is on-line. Tutorials for the noncomputer generation—those who did not grow up with computers in the classroom or the den, which at this point is most of us—should also be in hard copy, although they may have an interactive component.

Factors affecting the decision to implement electronic documentation include amount of memory available, cost, ease of updating, preferences of primary users, and potential need for translations into foreign languages.

ENVIRONMENTAL FACTORS

Creating on-line user guides is not done by transferring standard written material to a screen. It requires careful evaluation of factors unique to the interactive environment, incorporation of additional elements into the program's system design and the writing of the source program, and selection of the appropriate presentation style.

The unique environmental factors affecting interactive documentation include:

1   The hardware and user experience with the hardware

2   The screen formats

3   The relationship of the concepts of the data presented on any single display screen

4   The means for connecting related multiscreen data

Ergonomics is the study of the interrelationships between humans and their work environment and equipment. *Cognitive ergonomics* is a subcategory that covers working with concepts, such as the relationship between users and software. It is essential that documentation specialists stay current with developments in this field. Two journals in this area are *Ergonomics* and *Human Factors*. Much research already exists that is adaptable to user–display screen interface, but it has not been applied by the computer industry. Some of that data is included in this chapter.

Hardware

User experience with the hardware may be difficult to quantify, but if the initial project management steps are followed, data from the user profile should be sufficient to establish a range of user experience. It is important to provide information for both ends of the range. An interactive tutorial for a beginning user works well because it can easily be skipped over by a more experienced person.

Interface between the user and the system requires hardware-software coordination. For example, will certain keys, such as HELP or ?, be used to access data, or will it be accessed only through software, e.g., selecting from a help menu? Many systems use a combination. You must know the hardware specifications in order to design interactive user guides.

Screen Formats

There are two types of screen format parameters: (1) hardware controlled and (2) designer controlled. The hardware-controlled factors include such physical constraints as screen dimensions, program status line, and color of screen displays. Such factors should play a role in selecting the hardware on which your company's software will be used.

The designer-controlled factors include:

1 The spatial placement of characters on the screen

2 The display of characters and data (e.g., uppercase and/or lowercase letters and use of highlighting)

3 The manner in which data is grouped for easy reading and quick comprehension

An extensive study of screen formats was conducted by Thomas S. Tullis, of Bell Laboratories in New Jersey. Four types of CRT display formats for a computer-based, telephone-line testing system were evaluated. The four formats included: (1) narrative, (2) tabular, (3) black-and-white graphics, and (4) color graphics. Response times when using the two graphics formats were considerably shorter than those for the narrative format, and fewer training sessions were required to achieve the accuracy criterion. The subjective ratings also were considerably higher. Little difference was noted between black-and-white and color graphics, although Tullis notes that color could have become more important if the display had been more complex. The subjective ratings for color were higher and indicated it was pleasing and stimulating. The use of graphics was particularly effective for users with little experience. Users with more experience, however, could interpret displays in the tabular format just as effectively.

Conclusions of Tullis's study included the following:

1 Key information should be presented in a prominent location.

2 Logically related data should be physically grouped and separated from other categories of data.

3 Textual data should be presented in a fixed-column (tabular) format so that users develop spatial perceptions about location of data.

4 Information should be presented concisely.[1]

"Studies have shown repeatedly that human performance deteriorates with increasing display density."[2] Studies indicate that display density should not exceed 25 percent, although to date there is no definitive work that establishes a threshold density.

The following guidelines should be adhered to when designing display screens:

1 Text should be left-justified, numbers right-justified.

---

[1]Thomas S. Tullis, "An Evaluation of Alphanumeric, Graphic, and Color Information Displays," *Human Factors,* vol. 23, Santa Monica, Calif., 1981, pp. 541–550.

[2]Ibid., pp. 657–682.

2 If users are to select an item (from a menu, for example), the list should be presented vertically. Numbering should start with the number 1 and be left-justified.

3 Lists of information that do not require user selection should not be numbered. For fastest reading comprehension, the list should be presented vertically. Each item should be preceded by a bullet (lowercase letter *o*), asterisk, or other symbol, and subcategories should be indented farther.

4 A period should be used to indicate the end of a unit of data whether or not it is a complete sentence.

5 Sequential items should be presented from left to right and from top to bottom.

6 The status line of machine-generated data should be kept consistent and at a minimum.

7 Major headings may be in all caps, but text and other data to be read should be in uppercase and lowercase letters, just as a printed page would appear (lowercase letters are easier to read).

8 Similar data should be kept in the same location on different screens (for example, error messages should always be displayed in the same place).

9 Data presented on a screen should be kept to a minimum, and irrelevant data or instructions should not be included.

10 Data should be grouped into logical categories rather than presented as individual items.

Content

A series of screens is not a substitute for a book in which the eye can move easily from one page to the next. A screen must contain closely related information. Users cannot be referred back and forth to other screens, although they may progress through a hierarchical screen system for additional information as long as it is always clear what the relationships are and how to get back to the starting point. Nevertheless, interactive systems are fluid and dynamic, and users must always know where they are and how to move forward, backward, or out altogether (exiting).

Windows present a different set of design criteria. For example, how is data made visible, and how are windows accessed?

You must consider the information on one screen as a conceptual whole. If you have trouble with this, try giving it a heading and a goal statement, neither of which needs to be included on the screen. For example, a heading might be "Data entry screen for new inventory records." A goal statement for that screen might state, "The purpose of this display screen is: (1) to identify what task users are to complete; (2) to enable users to enter data in all required and optional fields to complete a new inventory record; and (3) to show users how to complete this entry and move to the next step, abort the entry and start again, or exit from the system." Note that it is not enough to use only the second part of that goal statement ("to enable users to enter data in all required and optional fields to complete a new inventory record") because, as stated earlier, users must know where they are in the system and how to move forward or backward.

One of the problems in selecting content for electronic documentation is remembering that you are telling users how to utilize the program, not how it works. This is true with hard-copy documentation also, but because of the close relationship between electronic documentation and the software, the writer may forget this distinction.

Multiscreen Connections

A hierarchical series of screens must be related in format and headings as well as content. In addition, users must be told on every screen how to progress forward, backward, or exit completely (and if they do exit, where they will end up). Headings for related screens should carry a similar major title followed by a subtitle for that specific screen. For example:

CHECK RECONCILIATION MAINTENANCE—INITIATION MENU

CHECK RECONCILIATION MAINTENANCE—ADD, CHANGE, DELETE PROCEDURES

CHECK RECONCILIATION MAINTENANCE—PURGE RECONCILED AND VOIDED CHECKS

CHECK RECONCILIATION MAINTENANCE—PRINT OPTIONS

Referring to a series of screens as CHECK RECONCILIATION MAINTENANCE—SCREEN 1 or CHECK RECONCILIATION MAINTENANCE, page 1, does not give users enough information. If a particular screen is more than one page long, the title should be repeated, followed by <u>Continued</u> and the page number. For example, CHECK RECONCIL-

IATION MAINTENANCE—ADD, CHANGE, DELETE PROCEDURES, page 1 (or page 1 of 2 pages); CHECK RECONCILIATION MAINTE-NANCE—ADD, CHANGE, DELETE PROCEDURES, Continued, page 2 (or page 2 of 2 pages).

Screen series should look alike. If diverse data is being displayed—such as a combination of text, lists, and entry screens—maintain a similar style for headings. Also ensure that terms are consistent and that format is the same where appropriate.

The most common conventions used in this chapter for examples of data entry instructions are as follows:

1　Keys are capitalized, e.g., press RETURN.

2　Names of display screens and menus in the text have the first letter of each word capitalized, e.g., the Tenant Record Data Entry Screen, the Tenant Rent Records Menu.

3　Names of screens and menus in a screen exhibit are presented as they appear on the actual screen.

4　All data, punctuation, and blank spaces entered by the user are underlined:

　　a.　Specified data to be typed is printed in bold and capitalized, e.g., enter **HELP**.

　　b.　Unspecified data or blank spaces are in parentheses, e.g., enter (your name), enter (1 space).

Use the same procedures for moving forward, backward, and exiting from each screen in the series and explain the options. "Enter **E** to End" or "Enter **X** to Exit" are too cryptic. What is ended? Where does one end up if exiting? Useful messages might state: "Enter **E** to return to the CHECK RECONCILIATION MAINTENANCE—INITIATION MENU," "Enter **X** to return to the PAYROLL SYSTEM MENU," "Enter **N** to move to the next screen," "Enter **P** to move to the previous screen." The last message would not appear on the first screen of the series, nor would the second-to-last message appear on the last screen of the series.

Always keep system messages or prompts in the same screen location—not just within a series of screens but throughout the system. Abbreviations may be used as long as they are consistent throughout the system and are identified completely in the first place in which users see them and in easily accessible accompanying written documentation.

TYPES AND STYLES

Types of electronic documentation, each of which will be discussed separately in the followlng sections, include:

1 Query-based help procedures

2 Key-based help procedures

3 Menus

4 Iconic (pictographic) menus

5 Prompting questions

6 Error message explanations

7 Interactive diagnostics

8 Interactive training, such as a tutorial

Query-Based Help Procedures

One example of help procedures documentation includes questions displayed by the system for users, such as, "Do you want additional information on how to do the merge-sort procedure?" with a *yes* or *no* response indicated. Another includes queries initiated by users, such as "Help Merge-sort."

If *yes* is entered for the first example, the system responds with a display screen containing concisely organized text material that explains the merge-sort procedures sequentially. This information is also displayed after the second example is entered.

Queries displayed by the system must be worded in a way familiar to users. If merge-sort procedures are consistently called by that name, do not write a query calling them the "merge and sort procedures," or the "combine/sort process." Consistent terminology is essential in creating a quality system.

If the query is system-generated, quantify and define the terms. For example, "Do you want additional information on merge-sort procedures?" is vague. What kind of additional information? How much additional information? Narrow the query to ask, "Do you want a list of step-by-step procedures for merge-sort?" or "Do you want an overview of the merge-sort process?" or "Do you want to know how to cancel or exit the merge-sort process?" If users have several options, use a menu rather than a single query.

If users are entering the query, ensure that the procedures are carefully explained, including not only data but spaces and terms to be used. For example, a hard-copy quick reference guide with a section on help options may accompany the system. It might state, "If you need additional information about the sequential procedures for any process during that process, enter **HELP** (*1 space*) (*the process name as it appears in the status line*) press RETURN. Valid process names are: merge-sort, alpha-sort, and numeric-sort."

Key-Based Help Procedures

These help procedures are tied directly to a keyboard with a HELP or ? key, which the users press. Depending on the system, users may or may not enter a word or phrase to define the area in which help is needed. Some systems can be structured so that information is given for the particular area of the program in which the user is working.

Written documentation accompanying the system must explain clearly the parameters for using a HELP key, i.e., how to define the area for which information is needed, the format of the information, and how much information can be requested.

Menus

Menus provide a list of options from which users may select one item at a time. The selection may lead to an additional menu or specific information. Menus often are used in hierarchical or tier structures, in which users move further into the system. In structuring menus, it is important to keep similar items together and to provide access forward and backward. See Exhibits 5-1a–d as an example of tiered (hierarchical) menus.

Notice that in the examples in Exhibits 5-1a–d, the title of the screen, the selection options, and the cursor position for entering data occur in the same place on each screen, even though the content of the information is different. On each screen, users have full information on moving forward, backward, or exiting and have access to a help menu that refers *only* to that particular screen. An example of a poorly written menu about three utility programs and the menu's improved alternative are shown in Exhibit 5-2.

The problems with the first menu include the following:

1 Vague title

2 List not justified

3 Inconsistent style for utility program names (i.e., QEDIT, Qedit)

4 Inconsistent style for describing content of each section (i.e., How to use, Step-by-step procedures)

5 Unequal treatment of content information (i.e., procedures for using QUERY and Qedit but only a list of uses for QUEST; also, no exit procedures for QUEST)

6 Lack of hyphenation in the phrase step-by-step procedures

7 No logical organization of information

Note that the second menu is organized alphabetically by the name of the utility program and that the list is left-justified. The reason for the two sections on exit procedures is that, for the purposes of this example, the QUEST exit procedures differ from those of QEDIT and QUERY.

Iconic (Pictographic) Menus

The use of iconics is a recent commercialized development in the computer industry. Users indicate the action to be taken by either pointing to a graphic representation of a specific action with a "mouse" or other handheld device for moving the cursor, moving the cursor by pressing

---

EXHIBIT 5-1(a)

Sample Tiered (Hierarchical) Menu: First Tier Menu Screen

SYSTEM FUNCTIONS MENU

1. Tenant Rent Records Menu

2. Accounts Receivable Menu

3. Transaction Types Menu

4. Tax Records Menu

5. Program Utility Systems Menu

6. Reports Menu

7. System Functions Help Menu

8. Exit the System

ENTER THE NUMBER OF YOUR SELECTION: _____
PRESS THE RETURN KEY

EXHIBIT 5-1(*b*)

Sample Tiered (Hierarchical) Menu: Second Tier Menu Screen

TENANT RENT RECORDS MENU

Select one of the following:

1. Enter new tenant records

2. Update existing tenant records

3. Enter utility bills

4. Enter cash receipts

5. Obtain reports on the display screen

6. Obtain printed reports

7. Access the Tenant Rent Records Help Menu

8. Return to the System Functions Menu (which enables you to select other system functions or exit the system)

ENTER THE NUMBER OF YOUR SELECTION: _____
PRESS THE RETURN KEY

EXHIBIT 5-1(c)

Sample Tiered (Hierarchical) Menu: Third Tier Menu Screen

PRINTED REPORTS SELECTION MENU

Select as many of the following reports as you wish to print:

1. Tenant List

2. Tenant Payment History

3. Gas Bills by Property

4. Electric Bills by Property

5. Cash Receipts for Month, Year, or Other Defined Range

6. Access to Tenant Rent Records Help Menu

7. Return to the Tenant Rent Records

8. Return to the System Functions Menu (which enables you to select other system functions or exit the system)

ENTER THE NUMBER(S) OF YOUR SELECTION(S): _____
PRESS THE RETURN KEY

EXHIBIT 5-1(*d*)

Sample Tiered (Hierarchical) Menu: Fourth Tier Menu Screen

GAS BILLS BY PROPERTY REPORT SELECTION SCREEN

Enter the data requested in steps 1 through 3 to define the selection criteria for Gas Bills by Property Report.

1   Enter the street, city, state, and zip code of the property(ies) for which you want to know the gas bills as indicated. You may select up to five properties at one time.

First Property Address _____

Second Property Address _____

Third Property Address _____

Fourth Property Address _____

Fifth Property Address _____

2   Enter the first date for which you want gas bills reported in MMYY format where indicated.

First Date: _____

3   Enter the last date for which you want gas bills reported in MMYY format where indicated.

Last Date: _____

4   To print the reports, press the PRINT key.

5   To return to the Tenant Rent Reports, press the RETURN key.

6   To return to the System Functions Menu, enter 6, press the RETURN key. (This menu enables you to select other system functions or exit the system.)

Enter 6 if you wish to return to the System Functions Menu: _____Then press the RETURN key.

EXHIBIT 5-2

Comparison of Poorly Written and Well-Written Menus

MASTER HELP MENU

1. How to use QUERY
2. Step by step procedures for QEDIT
3. How to exit most UTILITY PROGRAMS (Query, Qedit)
4. Uses for Quest

POORLY WRITTEN MENU

PROCEDURES FOR QEDIT, QUERY, AND QUEST HELP MENU

1. Step-by-step procedure information for QEDIT
2. Step-by-step procedure information for QUERY
3. Step-by-step procedure information for QUEST
4. Exit procedures for QEDIT, QUERY
5. Exit procedures for QUEST

WELL-WRITTEN MENU

---

cursor directional keys, or touching the screen. For example, if data entered is to be filed, there might be a picture of a file cabinet; if data is to be deleted, there might be a picture of a wastebasket.

One problem with iconics is that they take up a lot of screen space. A person who likes to work with a neat desk may think iconics add too much clutter to the screen (today's desk). Also, although drawn simply, iconics must convey a single possibility to *all* users. Confusing a wastebasket for a file cabinet could be disastrous.

Prompting Questions

Prompting questions should carry users through procedures and provide options at different points. For example, if users notice a mistake during data entry, they must have an opportunity to correct that mistake before moving on. A prompting question that would provide that option would be "Is the above information correct? Y/N." What happens when users enter Y or N must be clearly documented. This can be shown on the screen or in the hard-copy documentation.

Pitfalls to writing effective prompting questions include the following:

1 Using slang or a "cute" style that insults the users' intelligence and maturity. For example, "Naughty, naughty, you were supposed to enter your password on line 1. Now go back and do it correctly." Not only is the style nauseating, it does not even tell users how to go back and do it correctly.

2 Using incomplete or confusing instructions, for example, not telling users what really happens when they enter one of the options offered.

3 Using inconsistent procedures; for example, on one screen, entering **Y** may file the data and display the next screen; later, entering **Y** may take the user to another screen.

Error Message Explanations

Error message explanations and corrective actions lend themselves to electronic documentation if they are easily accessible by users and if access procedures are clearly described.

Error messages should be organized alphabetically (or numerically if the system gives each error message as a number that has to be decoded). Error messages that are numbers do not belong in interactive programs, or for that matter in any program that purports to be user friendly.

Electronic documentation of error messages can be set up in a table format. The message as it appears on the screen can be in the left-hand column, followed by a description of corrective action. If space allows, an example may be included.

Interactive Diagnostics

Automatic tellers and supermarket check approval computers are examples of how interactive diagnostics can be used. There is a "dialogue" between users and the computer to determine and complete specific tasks. Each step must be validated by the computer. Instructions for the next step are then given to users, even if this next step involves correcting the previous step. Careful coordination of the hardware and the instructions is essential.

Instructions must be unambiguous and readily understood by a variety of users. In some situations, displaying instructions near the area in which users are working might be helpful. For example, it might be useful to put a sign stating, "Enter your check in the check tray face-side up, with the check number in the upper right corner of the tray" on the screen above the check tray of a check approval computer. Ensure that the check tray is clearly marked Check Tray.

Interactive Training

A tutorial is an example of training material that can be written as an interactive program. If the system is designed for novice users, hard-copy documentation should accompany interactive tutorials.

One advantage of interactive training is that users can get immediate feedback on their actions. This concept is important in adult-learning theory. A good interactive training program takes advantage of this capability. Other than incorporating the instant-feedback factor, documentation specialists should write interactive training programs much as they would hard-copy training materials. The organizational logic is very important and must be established from the user's point of view. Also, more explanations are needed in tutorials than in other types of programs.

DEVELOPMENT CONSIDERATIONS

Time Frame and Staff Requirements

One difference between the development of electronic and hard-copy documentation is the time frame. Although writing electronic documentation may take as much elapsed time, it usually occurs earlier in the software development process. Electronic guides often are created in tandem with the system. Although hard-copy documentation should be developed this way, it rarely is. Documentation specialists must be involved in the development of electronic documentation. It should not be left to programmers unless they have been trained in writing this type of material.

With hard-copy user guides, you can select the type, style, and format of data presentation after the software programs have been developed. With on-line interactive systems, you usually select the type, style, and format of the interaction before the program has been completed. Specific content of the interaction between end users and the system is written simultaneously with the program. Thus close cooperation is necessary among systems designers, programmers, and documentation specialists.

One implication of this close cooperation is that the nature of on-line interactive documentation lends itself to a team approach. Writing hard-copy documentation can be an isolated task once the research has been completed. Writing interactive guides requires different skills and personal characteristics—such as a visual orientation and the ability to fit into a development team. It may not be possible for the same personnel to handle both jobs. The documentation department director must evaluate department personnel and adjust assignments accordingly.

In-house Review of Electronic Documentation

Reviewing electronic documentation is not the same as reviewing hard-copy user guides. You must educate your in-house reviewers about methods for conducting this type of review. You should supply an annotated "road map" to guide them through the process. This road map might consist of the following elements:

1 Clarification of what is expected of the reviewers, which should be standard procedure for any review but which requires more detail for electronic documentation reviews

2 Printouts of the material to be reviewed as well as the programs (if the reviewers have the means for running the programs)

3 A brief description of what is occurring, which should be enclosed in brackets and inserted between the electronic documentation comments

4 A checklist of the points the reviewers need to verify

ELECTRONIC PUBLISHING OF USER GUIDES

Electronic publishing, also called *down loading,* is one possible offshoot of electronic user guides. The document is written the way hard-copy material would be. It is then transferred to a magnetic medium (a diskette or a tape, for example) and is packaged with the software. End users load the electronic medium into the system and print the document. It is possible to design the documentation for interactive use too. Users load the electronic medium into the system and work with it on the terminal. In that case, the information is designed and written for interactive use. The latter example is particularly effective with tutorials and training programs.

Hardware compatability is essential, and communications configurations must be known in order to design the system. Also, it is essential to know whether end users will access the information on the terminal and/or print it.

With down loading, documentation specialists must do the following:

1 Ascertain how the table of contents, page numbers, and index can be kept intact

2 Ensure that any graphics can be properly communicated

3 Check the latest developments of the copyright law, which is in the process of changing, and its application to down loading

4 Provide explicit written instructions for accessing the down-loaded material

SIX

The Use of Graphics

In 1812, at the age of 21, Theodore Gericault was an up-and-coming artist and had a painting hung in the Paris Salon of that year. Several years later, he happened to be in Paris when the transport ship *Medusa* sank off the coast of Africa. The incident created great interest because of the scandalous behavior of the ship's officers, who commandeered the lifeboats. They left a crew of more than 100 to manage on a raft, which apparently the officers cast adrift. Weeks later, the raft was sighted by another ship and 15 crew members survived. Gericault was incensed and hired the ship's carpenter, one of the few survivors, to reconstruct the raft for him and describe in detail the ordeal. Gericault's concern for realism led him to borrow corpses from a nearby hospital to set the scene. This was too much realism for his neighbors, and he was forced to return his "involuntary models." The final painting was the violently animated work *The Raft of the Medusa,* which was shown at the Paris Salon of 1819. The critics abhorred it; the public was curious, but not the collectors. Bitterly resentful and vowing never to paint again, Gericault moved to England. Years after his death, the French government bought the painting, which is exhibited in the Louvre as the first example of Romantic Painting in the modern era.[1]

---

[1]Adapted text from *Enjoying Modern Art* by Sarah Newmeyer. Copyright © 1955 by Reinhold Publishing Corporation, New York, NY. All rights reserved.

Artists who attempt to depict reality have an easier time today, although their works are unlikely to end up in the Louvre. *Graphics,* an attempt to synthesize aesthetics and information (reality), is a type of art that evolved with our technical society. Although the Louvre may ignore this kind of art, the Museum of Modern Art in New York City does not; it includes a section on design and graphics.

Graphic displays traditionally have played an integral role in the creation of technical materials. Quantitative data, which technical writing often addresses, lends itself to visual presentation. In documentation, graphics—also called "visuals," "visual displays," or "visual aids"—are used in a variety of ways that go beyond the logical clustering of a series of numbers.

Presenting information graphically in documentation requires not only the inherent well-ordered logic of the technical writer but also the flair for the dramatic and the spatial perception of a designer. Nevertheless, the most important quality needed for incorporating graphics in documentation is neither logic nor drama. It is a needs-based approach to the categorization and organization of the data to be presented graphically.

The key to successful documentation is identifying, organizing, and presenting the information that the end users need in the order and manner in which they can use it most efficiently. This point is reemphasized because it has been the single greatest problem in producing workable documentation.

FRAMEWORK FOR SELECTING DOCUMENTATION GRAPHICS

Traditionally, the most common graphic display in software documentation has been the flowchart. The use of this device has been a mistake. The flowchart does not belong in user documentation unless the user is a programmer who will be making changes in the program. Rather, the flowchart provides raw data to be manipulated and shaped by the documentation writer.

Too often, a labyrinthian table or chart is inserted in the middle of a text simply because it has already been created. Its existence should not be an excuse for its use. The documentation writer must constantly make decisions about what and what not to use and how to use it. How are these decisions made? What are the guidelines for presenting data graphically?

Before setting priorities for presenting data graphically, it is necessary to refer to the project guide created as a documentation project management tool. The type of documentation needed sets the parameters for the use of graphics. For example, a user guide for a menu-driven program calls for graphic representations of the menus in the order in which users will access them. A manual for an off-the-shelf text-editing or word processing program that uses specific code keys for particular functions may use a graphic representation of the keyboard. The code keys would be highlighted, and a graphic-text combination of the sequential steps of the process would show the code keys and the action to be taken.

The first steps in determining what data to present graphically are reviewing the project guide, then examining the software program and identifying the data that lends itself to graphics. The documentation use must be kept clearly and constantly in mind. Graphics can help the documentation writer achieve the objectives of good technical writing: clarity, conciseness, and accuracy. Graphics can be used to emphasize a point, elaborate a concept, or attract interest.

The following guidelines may be used for selecting the type of data to be represented in a graphic display:

1 Comparisons

2 Visual representations of what the user will see at a specific time

3 Sequential processes with little or no explanatory text

4 Overview and interrelationships of system or program components

One means of verifying the selection of material is to ask the following questions:

1 Does use of this graphic display increase the effectiveness of the information?

2 Does use of this graphic display increase the efficient use of the information?

3 Does use of this graphic display provide the appropriate emphasis for the specific information that it is conveying?

The next step is ordering the data in the sequence in which it will be addressed by users of the guide. (Remember that the users may be defined as multiple target audiences.) Generally, this order will have been determined by the text outline of the document, which was discussed in Chapter 2. This is the basis for determining the specific use of graphics.

The motivating force behind the decisions about graphics is not the prior existence of certain tables, flowcharts, or diagrams. "But we've always used a flowchart in this manual!" is not an acceptable reason for continuing to do so. This does not mean that everything that has been done in the past is useless and should be ignored; but the specific realities defined for each individual project must govern the decisions about graphics use as well as style, format, and content of the text.

GRAPHIC DISPLAY TYPES AND STYLE GUIDELINES

Graphics for documentation uses can be categorized as follows:

1   Tables and figures

2   Graphs, including bar graphs, line graphs, pie charts, and pictograms

3   Diagrams, including flowcharts and process diagrams

4   Illustrations, including photographs and drawings

5   Computer screen representations

6   Computer printouts, including programs and program output

7   Forms, such as data entry forms

A computer graphics software program facilitates the use of graphics in documentation but is not a requirement. Most documentation graphics can be reproduced easily with a standard text-editing or word processing program.

General Style Considerations

Figures always appear as closely after the citation in the text as possible. In user documentation, the best practice is to have all information, whether text or graphics, presented on the page in the same reading direction. Graphics should not be placed sideways on a page. It is difficult to read and awkward to manage the document when one is following sequential instructions. Whenever possible, a figure should be contained on one page. If it takes up two or more pages, each succeeding page should contain the same heading and title as the original, followed by a comma and the word "Continued," e.g., "Figure 6-1, Continued."

Although standard technical writing differentiates between tables and figures, one approach to user documentation is to refer to all graphics as "figures," with the following three exceptions:

1   Computer printouts that are sample reports

2   Computer screen representations used throughout the text

3 Stand-alone figures, e.g., figures not integrated into the text, such as a data dictionary, which may have the heading "Data Dictionary" or "Field Descriptions"

One method for presenting the heading for figures or tables is the term "FIGURE" or "Figure," followed by the chapter or section number, a hyphen or decimal, and the sequential number of the figure in that particular section. The figure heading may appear one full line above or below the actual graphic. The line position may be controlled by format, binding considerations, and page design. The position selected must be consistent throughout the manual and related documents.

The title of the figure, with first letters of all important words capitalized, is centered one full line below the heading. Exhibit 6-1 is an example of the presentation of a figure.

Tables

Tables are used primarily for representing a series of numbers or items, making a comparison, or showing a relationship between two or more columns of numbers or items. A particularly useful table in many documentation situations is the cross-reference table. It relates one item to other types of items within a specific category, e.g., a record identification code that is used as a control in several fields. Exhibit 6-1 is an example of this type of table. Other commonly used types of tables are shown in Exhibits 6-2 and 6-3. Additional information on data dictionaries, another type of table, is given later in this chapter.

EXHIBIT 6-1

Accounts Payable Control Cross-reference Fields: Sample Figure

Use	Record ID Code	Fields				
		Date 1	Date 2	Date 3	Date 4	Voucher No.
Accounts payable/ processing date	AAP	Acctg. period	Processing date			Yes
Accounts payable/ release date	AAP	Acctg. period		Release date		Yes
Accounts payable/ record purge date	AAP				Purge date	No

FIGURE 2–1
Accounts Payable Control Fields Cross References

EXHIBIT 6-2

Spacing Codes: Sample Table

Key	Spacing Choice
1	Single spacing
2	Double spacing
3	Triple spacing
Q	Quarter-line spacing
H	Half-line spacing
T	Three-quarter-line spacing

A specific type of table used in the early days of computer programming was the decision logic table. It is rarely used today. This kind of table is based on the association or results of comparing two variables. For example, a decision logic table can be used by businesses to determinine withholding taxes. If an employee's salary is x, then the tax to be withheld is y. A decision logic table defines an if/then relationship. Some programmers and systems analysts continue to use this type of table, and, occasionally, it is a useful convention in documentation.

A decision logic table is divided into four quadrants (see Exhibit 6-4). Quadrant 1, the condition stub, contains the *if* statements dictated by the problem; quadrant 2 contains the actions or steps to be taken to solve the problem. Quadrants 2 and 4 may be subdivided into vertical columns called "rules." Quadrant 3 contains a *yes* or *no* response to indicate whether the condition exists for the circumstances represented by each column. Quadrant 4 contains a symbol to indicate whether action needs to be taken. The symbols most commonly used are a dash if no action is to be taken and an x if action is to be taken.

Tables are presented in vertical columns, although they may be printed sideways on a page if there are too many columns to fit across the page horizontally. If the vertical column headings are repeated, a table can be printed on side-by-side pages. This practice should be avoided whenever possible because it makes the end use of the document much less efficient. (Consider how difficult it is to turn a manual sideways when you are in the middle of a procedure.) Lines may be drawn vertically between the columns and should be drawn horizontally between the column headings and the column items. Lines are not needed to separate the items in a column.

Tables may be boxed, as in Exhibit 6-1, or left with open sides, as in Exhibit 6-3. The main consideration is consistency. Table titles should be concise but descriptive. Ensure that entries are aligned vertically and horizontally.

EXHIBIT 6-3

Data Dictionary: Sample Table

Field Name	Description	Alphanumeric/ Numeric	Print Length	Sample Field Value
ALPHASORT	Manufacturer name used for alphabetical sorting	A	25 variable	DCP MANUFACTURING
STATE	Manufacturer state	A	2 fixed	CO
STREET	Manufacturer street address	A	35 variable	10493 ST PAUL STREET
UNITDIM	Unit dimensions	N	6 variable	6.58 3.18 4.63
UNITWT	Weight of unit in pounds	N	6 fixed	120
TELNO	Manufacturer telephone number	N	12 fixed	303/555-1212

EXHIBIT 6-4

Quadrants in a Decision Logic Table

QUADRANT 1 Condition Stub	QUADRANT 2 Condition Entries
QUADRANT 3 Action Stub	QUADRANT 4 Action Entries

Figures

In documentation text, the heading "Figure" is used for most graphic displays. Exceptions include computer printouts; computer screen representations that are integrated into the sequential procedures; and stand-alone figures with their own headings, such as a data dictionary. In the world of graphic design, the term "figure" also refers to a specific type of graphic, which can best be defined by what it is not. A figure is not a table, a graph, a printout, or a form. Figures may represent various types of information. In a sense, they are the miscellaneous category of graphics. Exhibit 6-5 shows how a figure might be used in documentation and integrated with the text.

The figure heading and title are placed below the actual figure. Figures, like tables, may or may not be boxed. Again, consistency is the principal consideration.

EXHIBIT 6-5

Sample Figure Integrated with Text

The superscript/subscript feature of this text-editing program facilitates the entering of complex chemical formulas and mathematical calculations. See Figure 1-2.

$$C_{10}H_4NH_2OH(SO_3H)_2$$

$$P_0(x)y^n + P_1(x)y^{n-1} + \ldots + P_{n-1}(x)y + P_n(x) = 0$$

Figure 1-2

Sample Superscript/Subscript Feature

Bar Graphs

The most common types of bar graphs are horizontal, vertical, and component graphs. They are used to show a relationship between quantitative data with one dependent variable and one independent variable. Bar graphs are used more frequently as a management tool than in documentation materials. Exhibit 6-6 is an example of a vertical bar graph, Exhibit 6-7 shows the same information as a horizontal bar graph, and Exhibit 6-8 is an example of a component bar graph.

Another way of presenting the data in Exhibit 6-8 is to put the cost category symbols, i.e., ▥ Overhead, ▨ Staff & Consultants, and □ Production, in one of the upper corners and to list the dollar amounts in increments of $1000 vertically on the right side of the graph.

Generally, the dependent variable is vertical and the independent variable is horizontal, as in Exhibit 6-6. If symbols or abbreviations are used, they are included in the rectangular space of the graph, usually in one of the upper corners.

Pictograms

Pictograms are bar graphs using simple graphic sketches of the item that is being measured in place of the bars. Each pictogram represents a certain number of items. Exhibit 6-9 is an example of a pictogram.

Each pictogram must represent the same number of units throughout the graph. However, it is possible to use a part of the drawing to represent a fraction of that multiple unit, as the data for 1983 does in Exhibit 6-9. Pictograms add interest to a document and can be used to good ad-

EXHIBIT 6-6

Number of Text-Editing User Manuals Released, 1980–1983: Sample Vertical Bar Graph

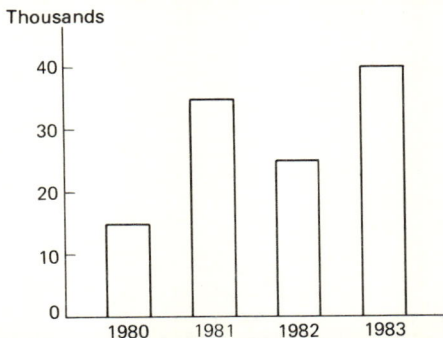

EXHIBIT 6-7

Number of Text-Editing User Manuals Released, 1980–1983: Sample Horizontal Bar Graph

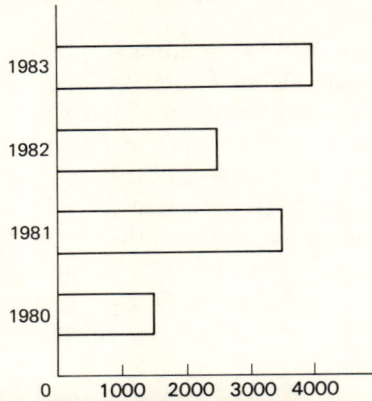

EXHIBIT 6-8

Costs of Producing Text-Editing User Manuals, 1982–1983: Sample Component Bar Graph

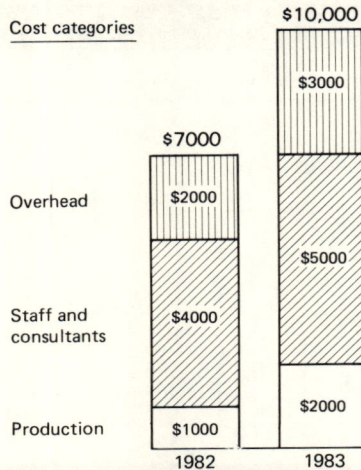

EXHIBIT 6-9

Floppy Diskette Sales, 1981–1983: Sample Pictogram

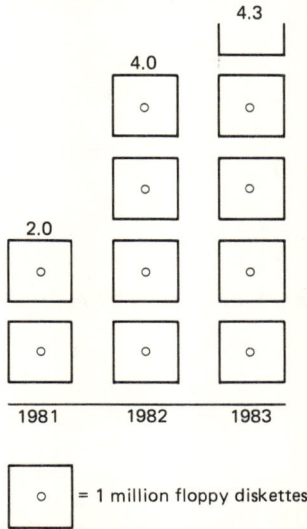

vantage in promotional material, annual reports, and professional presentations.

Line Graphs

Line graphs are used to show a trend or relationship between two variables, one of which is usually time. As with bar graphs, they are used primarily as a management tool. Exhibit 6-10 is an example of a line graph.

The time variable is listed horizontally at the bottom of a line graph. Note that the sequential variable listed vertically on the left of the graph does not need to start with zero. Another possible feature is writing the numbers represented at the key points (peaks and valleys) of the graph. Generally, this would be done only when depicting large numbers with a wide range between the vertical variables.

Pie Charts

Pie charts show the relationship of parts to the whole. Exhibit 6-11 is a hypothetical example of the results of one question in a company market survey.

EXHIBIT 6-10

Production Time for Technical Documentation, 1980–1983: Sample Line Graph

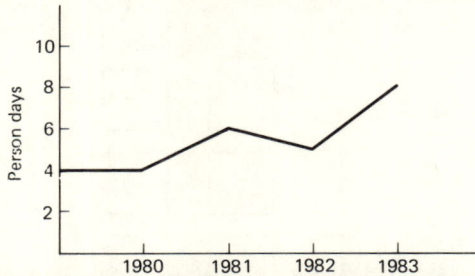

The sum of the parts equals 100 percent in a pie chart. The segments are arranged according to size; the largest is first and begins at 12 o'clock. The percentage amount and an identification name should be included in each segment. If the segment is too small, the information can be printed outside the circle, with an arrow to the appropriate segment, as with the "Database Management" and "Don't Know" segments in Exhibit 6-11. The raw data figures may be included in each segment if that information is useful and can be added without crowding the diagram.

EXHIBIT 6-11

Next Software Package To Be Purchased, Market Survey Results, 1985: Sample Pie Chart

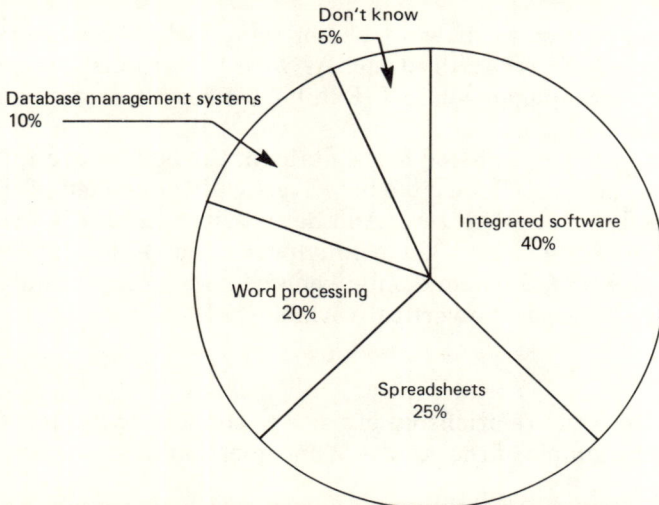

Flowcharts

Flowcharts are a precise and commonly used tool in program development documentation and technical documentation. They should rarely appear in user documentation. A flowchart carries information regarding what program or operation occurs as a result of which preceding step. It does not describe how users can make it happen, why it happens, or when it happens in terms of the user's perspective.

To be understood, a flowchart must utilize established symbols and conventions. Flowchart format is set by the American National Standards Institute (ANSI). Flowchart templates are available. If a template is not used, it is essential that not only the shape but the relative size and proportion of the symbols be maintained.

Industry uses two types of flowcharts: system charts and flow diagrams. A *system chart* (also called a "system flowchart" or "run diagram") comprises the sequential operational steps of a program. These charts start with input, proceed through process, and end with output.

The *flow diagram* is a microscopic look at one section of a system flowchart. It gives the details that are ignored with the broader brush strokes of a system flowchart. As a result, it often appears more complex. Another way of looking at the flow diagram is to consider it a graphic depiction of an algorithm.

There are entire books written on flowcharting, but the most common standard conventions can be summarized. The flow direction reads from left to right and from top to bottom, as one would read a normal page of print. Deviations from the normal flow direction are shown with arrows. Annotations are connected by a dotted line and partially enclosed by three sides of a rectangle.

Process Diagrams

The concept of process diagrams was created by the author to meet the need for expressing sequential operations in a graphic format that was less formalized and had a more user-oriented emphasis than a flowchart. Process diagrams are particularly useful for detailed promotional material and user documentation. They may be drawn for an entire program to give an overview of the system, which is called a "system process diagram." Process diagrams may also be drawn to show a specific sequential series of operations that forms a logical subunit of the program in terms of user interaction. This is called an "operations process diagram."

The symbols used are not governed by national standards. However, it is recommended that consistent symbols be used because they enhance understanding of the content of process diagrams. The sample symbols shown here can be created by any simple graphics function on a word processor; a template is not required. The size of the forms can be adjusted to fit the inserted labels and space available, but the shape and relative size should be kept intact. See Exhibit 6-12 for sample process diagram symbols. Exhibit 6-13 presents a system process diagram, and Exhibit 6-14 presents an operations process diagram.

As with flowcharts, process diagrams are read from left to right and top to bottom. Arrows indicate deviations from the direction of the normal flow of information, although they may be used throughout, as in Exhibit 6-13. Connectors are used to indicate a break in the flow, such as the end of a line and the beginning of a new line. The connector 1A in Exhibits 6-13 and 6-14 is an example. Annotations may be added, such as those enclosed in brackets in Exhibits 6-13 and 6-14.

The key to a useful process diagram is the conceptualization of the steps being depicted. The diagram designer must look at the program from the point of view of potential users and break out the action components. These components may be one or more steps in the actual program. They can be categorized as user decisions or input, processing

EXHIBIT 6-12

Process Diagram Symbols

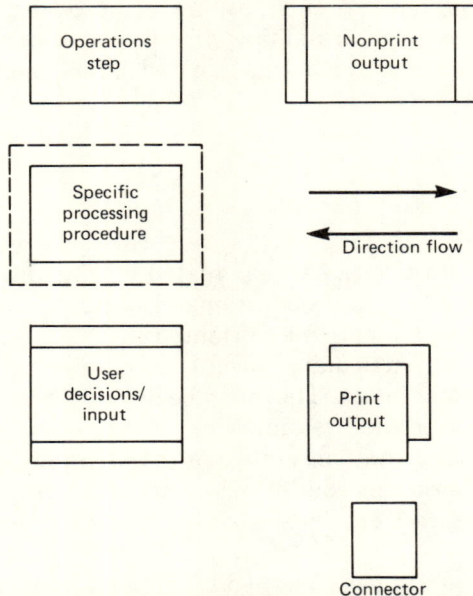

EXHIBIT 6-13

(a) H-A Software Payroll System; (b) Sample System Process Diagram

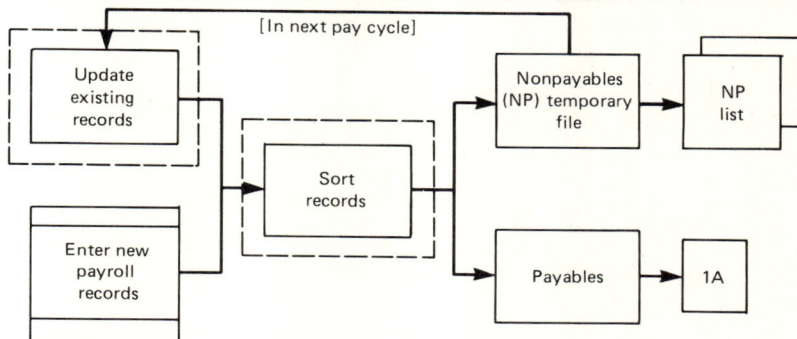

(a)

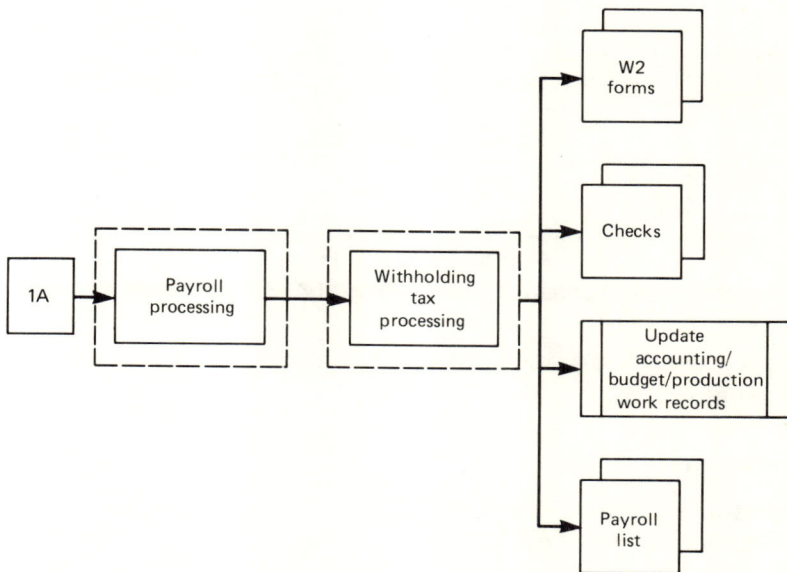

(b)

EXHIBIT 6-14

H-A Software Energy Control System—Electric Meter Monitor Subsystem: Sample
Operations Process Diagram

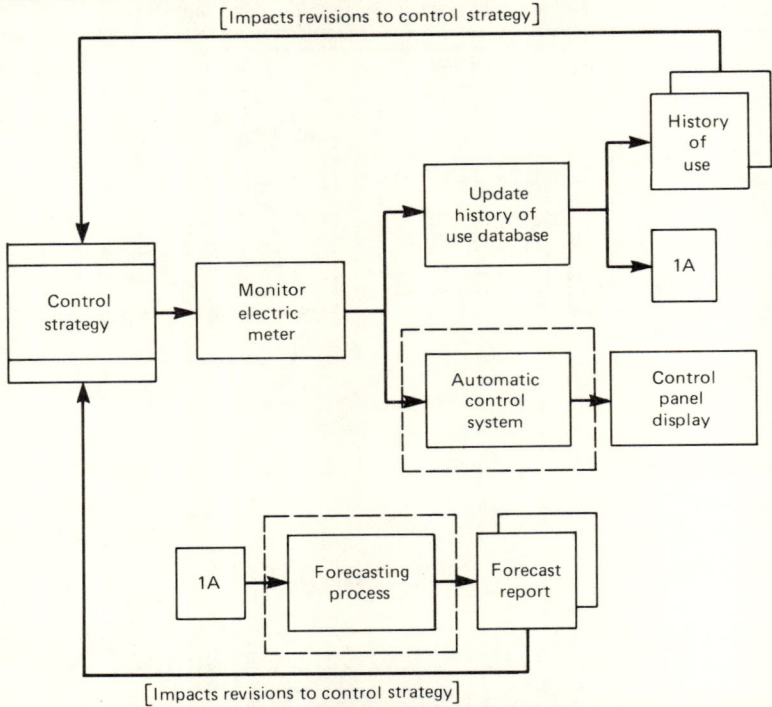

procedures, operations steps (nonprocessing procedures), nonprint output,
and print output.

Illustrations

Photographs, line sketches, and drawings may be used in software documentation but are found more commonly in hardware documentation.
They are labeled as figures, and the conventions and requirements for
figures apply.

Computer Screen Representations

A representation of a computer screen is perhaps the most commonly used
graphic in software documentation. There are no established industry

standards to date. Using a rectangle with the number of spaces (width) and number of lines (length) of the actual screen is the most useful format.

The screen representation must be delineated in a clear way. The most common technique is to box it. Also, reverse printing may be used, i.e., the screen background area is dark and the printing is light. This method can be effective, but ensure that the contrast and the printing quality is adequate for legibility. Do not print screen representations so small that they cannot be easily read.

Screen representations are effective in user documentation at those points at which the user accesses the screen. They are beneficial for depicting menus, location of messages, status line requirements, and prompts.

If screen representations are a continually repeated aspect of the documentation presentation, they do not need to be labeled as figures. Instead, they should come under a standard subsection heading with proper specific identification. Nevertheless, if only one or two representations are to be used—for example, to show what the status line looks like in a text-editing program—they should be labeled as figures. The conventions and standards for figures should then be used. Exhibit 6-15 is a typeset copy of a computer screen representation of a menu for accessing an information network database. In this particular system, users access the screen repeatedly; therefore, screen representations would carry section or subsection headings, e.g., Menu 1 User Notebooks.

EXHIBIT 6-15

Network Resources Notebook Menu: Sample Computer Screen Representation

MENU 1 USER NOTEBOOKS

```
                    WELCOME TO THE NOTEBOOKS


    Please do one of the following:

        —  Type the entire name of a notebook
        —  Type any word in the name of a notebook
        —  Type the word 'ALL' to see a list of all the
              notebooks
        —  Type a '?' for an explanation of these choices
        —  Press the Return or New Line key to stop

    Type here >
```

Source: Courtesy of Lief Smith, Network Resources, Denver, Colorado

Computer Printouts

Computer printouts may show either output or a particular part of a program. They are commonly used in all types of documentation. How they should be presented is a difficult question. Computer printouts usually are not easy to read. The best approach is not to include actual printouts in documentation unless they are being used as sample reports. In that case they are useful because what the user sees is exactly what the user gets. Almost without exception, the information given in other printouts can be presented in a better manner in text or with graphics.

If printouts must be used, ensure that they are originals, printed on clean paper with no shading. Printouts may be presented as figures or stand-alone graphics, depending on content and use. Whichever form is used, the standard conventions for headings and spacing apply.

Forms

The most common forms in documentation are input, or data entry, forms. Such forms duplicate the originals as closely as possible. Each entry field

EXHIBIT 6-16

Personnel Record Entry Form: Sample Input Form

Name 1
Street address 2
Additional street address 3
City 4   St 5
Zip 6   Telephone 7   Dept. code 8
SS number 9   Insurance plan number 10
Start date 11   Term date 12   Term code 13
Job description code 14
Job description 15
Most recent performance review codes 16
Previous performance review codes 17

EXHIBIT 6-17

Data Dictionary by Field Name

Field Name	English Name	Alphanum. (A) /Numeric (N)	Field Length	System Codes	Sample or Decode
AREA	Square Footage	N	10		10000
BLDGT	Building Type	A	45		Apartment
PRICE	Purchase Price	N	10		1250000
PURCHASE	Date Purchased	N	6		091084 (MMDDYY format)
TNTNAME	Tenant Name	A	45		DHA Software Inc
TNTTYPE	Tenant Type	A	3	1,2,3	1 = Apartment Tenants 2 = Office Tenants 3 = Warehouse

is numbered sequentially on the form and in the corresponding text instructions. Exhibit 6-16 depicts a simple input form that might be used for personnel records.

Data Dictionaries (Field Descriptions)

Data dictionaries, also called "field descriptions" or "field explanations," are tables that list specific information about the user-entered data fields. They represent an excellent use of the graphic display of information in user manuals. They provide clear, concise, easy-to-locate information that is essential to the data entry person.

Depending on how the information is used, the first column would be the field name—if that is how users will look it up—or the English name of the field. Sometimes both tables are needed. The entries are almost always alphabetical. A segment of a data dictionary with the field name first is shown in Exhibit 6-17, and with the English name first in Exhibit 6-18. Note that in the second example, the information is categorized. This is not a requirement but would be dictated by the number of fields being described and the complexity of the information. Another data dictionary example is shown in Exhibit 6-3.

INDEPENDENT GRAPHIC DISPLAYS

Quick Reference Cards

These user guides come in a variety of formats. They may be any size and are usually printed on glossy, heavy paper that will hold up to fre-

EXHIBIT 6-18

Data Dictionary by English Name

English Name	Field Name	Alphanum. (A) /Numeric (N)	Field Length	System Codes	Sample
BUILDING DATA					
Building Type	BLDGT	A	45		Apartment
Square Footage	AREA	N	10		10000
PURCHASE DATA					
Date Purchased	PURCHASE	N	6		091084 (MMDDYY format)
Purchase Price	PRICE	N	10		1250000
TENANT DATA					
Tenant Name	TNTNAME	A	45		DHA Software Inc
Tenant Type	TNTTYPE	A	3	1,2,3	1 = Apt. Tenants 2 = Office Tenants 3 = Warehouse

quent use. They might range from a 10- by 16-inch format, folded in four sections, or the size of playing cards with separate information on each card, organized on a key ring attached to the computer terminal.

The essence of quick reference cards is to provide the key information the user needs. This information is specific to each software system. It could be command entries, error messages, system codes, or default codes, for example. These cards usually are designed for experienced users; therefore, explanations rarely are given. Be sure to group information logically for easy access, and use large, clear headings for each section of data. If possible, use the services of a graphic designer once you know what content is to be included. The actual design is more difficult than designing a page layout or creating a system process diagram.

During the design process, keep in mind the following criteria:

1 Adequate white space

2 Legibility

3 Logical groupings

4 Relevant information

5 Easy access to the information

6 Effective headings

Posters

Posters can be very effective for providing quick reference material for experienced users, giving new users an overview of the system, or providing management with information on what a system can accomplish. The first question is to know the work environment. Is it likely that the posters will be hung so that the information they contain is accessible to the people who need it? This usually is the greatest deterrent to using posters.

A graphic designer should be used to design the final poster. Nevertheless, you can determine the content and the flow of information. A poster provides dynamic movement to the information it contains. Take advantage of that, and use it to enhance the content. The same criteria for quick reference cards apply to posters, but the arrangement and type of information to be displayed will be different. There are no set rules, which is one reason why a trained designer is essential. Study other posters and full-page magazine and newspaper ads to get ideas of what works and does not work. Work closely with the printer on the final production. The actual printing can determine whether a poster succeeds or fails, providing it was well designed initially.

PRODUCTION OF GRAPHICS

Ideally, a graphic designer will be included on the documentation project team as a staff person, consultant, or contractor. Frequently, this person will also provide layout and production expertise. In cases in which such a person is not available, the documentation specialist can complete the graphic design requirements. If the documentation specialist is going to assume these responsibilities, adequate time must be allocated for these tasks.

Equipment and supplies needed include the following:

1 Light table

2 Graph paper

3 Black pens with different point thicknesses

4 Drawing pencils

5 Artgum or similar eraser

6 Templates for required shapes

7 Exacto knife

8 Glue stick or rubber cement

9 Transfer letter sheets and tapes, e.g., Letraset or Chartpak

10 Ruler

11 Correction fluid

12 Quality bond paper

13 Masking tape

It is best to start with a rough sketch of your graphic display that includes all the content data. Be sure that your numbers and other information are accurate before you start work on the actual design. Check the location of the graphic in the text, and coordinate the space allowed with your design. Be sure to leave room for any headers, footers, titles, symbol explanations, and references. These can be typed and stripped in later.

Using the ruler and templates, mark out the space allotted on a sheet of graph paper taped to the light table. Lay out the graphic in pencil, then write or block in any information in the print size you want to use. This is your model; not the final copy. Check your design again with the space allotted, verify the content data, and make any corrections.

Now you are ready to do your final copy. Tape graph paper to the light table again. This time use black pens for all lines. Take extra care to keep your work neat and accurate. When the pen work is completed and dry, tape a sheet of bond paper over the graph paper and trace the design with a drawing pen on the bond. Use the transfer sheets and chart tapes to add special effects, keeping the graph paper under the bond to use for reference points. You can add typed text by cutting it with the Exacto knife and gluing it in place.

When you have finished, keep the graphic between two sheets of clean paper until you are ready to insert it in the camera-ready manuscript. At that point, remove the protective sheets. Be sure that the graphic, if it is to be a separate page, is numbered correctly. If it is to be placed on another page, put that page over a sheet of graph paper taped to the light table. Cut the graphic to fit with the Exacto knife. Use glue stick or rubber cement to attach the graphic in place, checking the graph paper to ensure that the alignment is correct.

SEVEN

Editing, Review, and Evaluation Procedures

There are six types of editing, review, and evaluation procedures:

1 Proofreading

2 Editing

3 Technical review

4 Beta tests

5 User surveys

6 Industry evaluation

The first three are in-house procedures. The fourth is monitored by the company although testing is by end users; the fifth is also monitored by the company but the evaluation is by end users. The sixth is independent industry reviews.

Proofreading, editing, and technical review are essential for creating effective user guides. Each should be done at a specific point in the development cycle. Because of the time frame under which user guides usually are produced, these steps frequently are short-circuited. This may be the single most important reason why many user materials are substandard.

Beta tests are a hybrid form of review and evaluation. They occur after prototype development and before widespread commercial release of a new system. A limited number of potential end users are selected to try out the system. It is expected that there will be problems to be resolved.

Nevertheless, it is in the best interest of the future marketability of the product to keep problems at a minimum during the Beta tests.

User surveys and industry evaluation occur after the development and distribution of a system in the marketplace. End-user surveys are conducted by the company, usually with a specific questionnaire. Industry evaluation may be done independently by software distribution companies and trade journals.

PROOFREADING

Proofreading (or *proofing*) is the word-by-word, line-by-line examination of a manuscript for typographical errors, such as missing characters, incorrect characters, and information that may have been omitted by the typist. Ideally, proofing should be a two-step process. The first step should be done by the typist, who places the original manuscript and the typed copy side by side and skims them to ensure that no material has been omitted. Obvious typographical errors (typos) can be caught at this time. Approximately 20 double-spaced pages can be skimmed for omissions in one hour.

The second step should be done by someone who did not do the typing. This is a line-by-line review for typos and other obvious errors. The reason for having another person perform this task is that our brains play tricks on us. You know the word is supposed to be "receipt," for example, but you accidentally typed it "reciept." When you read the copy, unless you are very careful, you may see the word properly spelled. Even the best editors have other people proof their typed copy.

Common proofreading symbols are presented in Exhibit 7-1, and a sample proofed page is shown in Exhibit 7-2.

EDITING

There are two types of editing, both of which are essential: (1) editing for style and format and (2) editing for content.

Style and Format

A project or company stylebook is invaluable for organizing this type of editing. Simple checklists in the following categories can be developed and used for a multiple-pass editing process. If your company does not

EXHIBIT 7-1

Proofreading Symbols

	Symbol	Description
		Delete
		Delete and close up
	□	Quad (one em) space
	⊔	Move down
	⊓	Move up
	⊏	Move to left
	⊐	Move to right
eq #		Equalize spacing between words
×		Broken letter
¶		Begin a new paragraph
no ¶		No new paragraph
stet		Let type stand as set
(?)		Verify or supply information
tr		Transpose letters or marked words
sp		Spell out (abbrev.) or (7)
∪		Push space down
=		Straighten type
‖		Align type
run in		Run in material on same line
bu		Change (x/y) to built-up fraction
sh		Change x/y to shilling fraction
		Set as subscript
		Set as exponent

Symbol	Description
lc	lowercase Word
cap	Capital letter
sc	SMALL CAPITAL LETTER
bf	Boldface type
ital	Italic type
rom	Roman (type)
wf	Wrong font
#	Insert space
⊃	Close up
9	Turn letter
⊙	. Period
⌃	, Comma
⌄	' Apostrophe
⌵⌵	" " Quotation marks
;/	; Semicolon
⊙	: Colon
?/	? Question mark
!/	! Exclamation mark
=/	- Hyphen
⌁	– En dash
⌁	— Em dash
⌁	—— Two-em dash
(/)/	( ) Parentheses
[/]/	[ ] Brackets

have a stylebook, you must create the checklists. A one-pass, line-by-line attempt to catch all errors does not work.

Each of the following questions should be examined in a separate review or pass of the entire manuscript. This system of using one complete pass to check one type of information is the only way to ensure an error-free product. The questions include the following:

1 *Location accuracy:* Are the table of contents, list of figures and tables, headers and footers, and headings correct in terms of what they describe, in form, and in style (capitalization and punctuation)?

2 *Front and back matter:* Is everything included in the proper sequence; is the information complete; are grammar and punctuation correct?

3 *Lists:* Is the format correct; are the elements parallel?

4 *Tables, figures, and computer printouts:* Are the titles correct; is the graphic needed; is it referred to correctly in the text; is the format correct?

EXHIBIT 7-2

Sample Proofed Page

---

bf   Formulating Questions

tr   To develop a competitive documentation strategy, you must build your fundation.
tr   The first question any executive must ask is, "What is our business?" Then
     consider related questions: "What is the purpose of the company?" "Is the company
ℓ   in production or distribution?" "Is the company's strong suit innovative new
     programs that need a lot of Beta testing or standard workhorse programs?" "Is the
     business changing?" "If not, should it be changing?" You can see how one question
ℓ   leads rapidly to another. Before you find yourself in a maze, organize your
     questions.

Questions can be formulated under the following categories:

ℓ   1   Corporate goals,
cap/ℓ 2   market positioning,
ℓ   3   Market definition,
ℓ   4   Competition,
ℓ   5   Corporate strengths,
ℓ   6   Corporate weaknesses and implications of those weaknesses,
#/ℓ 7   Potential revision of corporate goals in light of data collected during analysis.

---

5 *Text:* Are the grammar, punctuation, and format correct; does it read
clearly; is any jargon used; are unfamiliar terms explained?

Exhibit 7-3 is an example of a checklist for one pass for editing lists.

EXHIBIT 7-3

Checklist for Editing Lists

List Conventions	O.K.
Lead-in from text	
Correct tab and indention (indent 5 for number, 10 for text, second line at 10 also)	
Sequential numbers	
Capitalization (first letter)	
Punctuation (none unless each item is a complete sentence, then use periods)	
Parallel elements	

Content

Content editing concerns the actual information given rather than the manner in which it is presented. The editor becomes the future user of the manual. In this role, the editor is representing the reader's interface with the manual just as the documentation writer is representing the reader's interface with the software system.

The following questions should be asked when reviewing a manuscript's content. This list is meant as a guide; additional questions may be appropriate for the specific manual you are editing:

1 Is the organization logical for the user?

2 Is equal weight given to equal topics?

3 Is the information complete?

4 Is irrelevant information included?

5 Is the information technically accurate?

6 Are the instruction procedures correct?

7 Are graphics used appropriately?

8 Are additional graphics needed?

9 Is terminology correct?

10 Are unusual terms or system-specific terms defined?

11 Is each component of information given the correct emphasis?

12 Are the transitions from one section to another effective?

13 Are the goals and objectives clearly defined and reasonable?

14 Does the manual meet the stated goals and objectives?

15 Is the audience orientation correct?

16 Are concepts clear?

17 When you read each section aloud, does it make sense?

Answering these questions can be accomplished only by becoming familiar with the user profile and then reading and rereading the manuscript. It is not possible to answer all these questions with one reading.

One effective editing technique is to review this list after reading each section or chapter and to check off a yes or no response. A matrix table with the essential phrases from the questions listed vertically and

EXHIBIT 7-4

Content-Editing Matrix Table

	System Overview	System Access	Hardware Interface	Tutorial	Sequential Procedures	Commands	Messages
Organization logic							
Equal weight for equal topics							
All information							
Irrelevant information							
Accuracy							
Procedures correct							
Graphics use							
More graphics							
Terminology correct							
Terms defined							
Emphasis correct							
Transitions							
Goals stated							
Goals met							
Audience orientation							
Concepts clear							
Makes sense							

the manual sections listed horizontally provides an easy tool for keeping track of content editing. A quick look will indicate problem sections and patterns of specific problems throughout the manuscript. Exhibit 7-4 is a sample content-editing matrix table.

The major issue with content editing is rewriting. How far can and should the editor go in revising a manuscript? How do you discuss major revision problems and proposed revisions with writers?

Theoretically, less ego involvement should occur in technical writing than in creative writing or even journalistic writing. As many battle-scarred editors will tell you, this is not always the case. The key to how far the editor should go with revisions—either completed by the editor or requested from the writer—can be based on the stated project goals. These provide an objective measure by which an editor can identify and request required changes.

The decision whether the editor or the writer will do major rewrites should be based on several variables. These include the length of the material to be rewritten, the preestablished responsibilities for rewrites, the knowledge of the editor about the subject matter, and the time that the editor and the author have available for rewrites.

Occasionally issues concerning writing style will arise. The writer may have presented the material correctly, but the editor may feel it could be presented more clearly. The most effective way to deal with these problems is in the form of a question. For example, the editor might write in the margin, "Do you think 'alternative approach' works better here? If not, what about 'another suggested option?' "

The way in which a project is managed can make a big difference in the relationship between the editor and the writer. A project team approach with preestablished written responsibilities for each team member will make the editor's role easier. A commitment from management to quality documentation also enhances the editor's work. Finally, if the editor is well-organized, presents necessary changes at one time, and documents (as required) the need for those changes, the relationship between the writer and editor can contribute to effective user guides.

TECHNICAL REVIEW

The technical review phase is concerned specifically with the accuracy of the content of the user guides. There are two primary means for checking for this: (1) test the manual yourself or have it tested by a subordinate by going through the system with the manual to see if explanations are complete and accurate, and (2) request manuscript review by the systems analysts or programmers who designed the system.

User-Simulation Testing

Testing the manual as a potential user is an excellent means of checking accuracy, organization, and presentation of information. This requires personnel and hardware. It is most effective if you have the manual checked by someone who did not participate in developing the document. Ask the "new user" to start at the beginning, with system entry. Provide a questionnaire to verify results. Design your questions to reflect the specific system. Sample questions include the following:

1   Please time how long it takes you to figure out initial system access. Amount of time: _____.

2   What is the purpose of this system?

3   Was the table of contents comprehensive? Accurate?

4   What task(s) did you complete?

5   Where did you find the information to help you complete this (these) task(s)?

6   Was the manner in which information was organized helpful?

7   Could you locate needed information quickly?

8   Was the information accurate?

Review by Programmers

Too often, programming staff are under difficult time pressures. An additional task, especially one including a review of a project they have probably completed, is a resented intrusion.

Select technical reviewers carefully. Because reviewers must be able to ascertain whether the content of the manual is accurate, they must be people who either wrote the programs, supervised the writing of the programs, or were closely involved with the development of the system. It is best not to give the entire manual to one person. Chances are that person would have time to do only a superficial job.

Select your reviewers early in the project and write them memos asking their cooperation. Give them a tentative schedule of when they can expect to receive the sections they must review. Tell them how long they will have to complete the review. Include a statement from their supervisor giving approval for completion of this task. Never give them the last date by which you must have the material back; always allocate some contingency time. Keep them apprised as the project moves along. One to two weeks before you send them the manuscript for review, you

EXHIBIT 7-5

Checklist for Technical Reviewers

Personnel Records System User Manual Section III. Personnel Record Entry	OK	Comments
Procedures sequentially correct Specific screen entry procedures accurate Data entry procedures accurate All exit procedures included and accurate Error messages stated as they appear Field lengths accurate for user-entered data All field defaults included and accurate All field system codes included and accurate All required and key fields noted		
Additional Comments:		

Signature

Date

should confirm their participation in writing, reiterate your schedule, and briefly describe the process.

Include specific instructions for each review and a checklist of the kinds of things for which you want them to look. Also include any specific questions you have. Exhibit 7-5 is an example of this type of checklist. Enclose a form stating that the manuscript is technically accurate as corrected with a place for the reviewer's signature and the date. Ask the reviewer to return this to you with the corrected copy.

BETA TESTS

Traditionally, documentation has been written after systems have been developed and tested. This is a mistake. Documentation should be created simultaneously with the programs. If documentation is developed in this fashion, it can be tested during program testing. Three major benefits result from this timetable:

1 The test can serve as a check to ensure that the documentation is accurate and useful.

2 The documentation can provide a framework for the testing and facilitate the testing.

3 The documentation can serve as a check to ensure that the programs are working properly.

USER SURVEYS

Perhaps you have developed and implemented your project management plan; you believe all your data is accurate and your decisions reasonable. The manuals have been produced and distributed, and you have started on the next project.

Wait a minute. Is that all there is to it? What image is your documentation projecting—not to you, the marketing-sales staff, or your public relations consultants—but to the end users, the customers? Are they using the documents in the ways you expected? Do they need additional information? Have they learned shortcuts that you should pass on to less experienced users?

If you are documenting off-the-shelf software, you can reach your market by enclosing a prepaid mailer and a questionnaire in the package. Questions must be short and specific if you want to get answers.

If you know your client audience, you can conduct a user survey. Know what information you want to learn before you design your questionnaire. Use the following steps to design and implement a documentation-evaluation survey:

1 Determine what you want to learn, for example, whether a specific manual is easy to use or whether a specific approach or presentation enables a new user to learn data entry.

2 Identify the target audience.

3 Determine the survey methodology. (What user demographics will be important—length of time on the system, prior training? What percentage of the target audience represents an adequate sample? Which specific users should be surveyed?)

4 Develop the questions and rating scale.

5 Conduct the survey.

6 Quantify the responses.

7 Determine the conclusions.

8 Use the conclusions to improve documentation products.

The last step is crucial to the entire evaluation effort. Do not just collect feedback; use it to improve your products. Look at suggestions that are made and tie them directly to the user guides you are distributing. For example, you might get a complaint from data entry personnel that, when they are sitting at the terminal, they do not have time to thumb through a thick manual to find a specific procedure that they have forgotten. Possible responses could be data entry sections in different colors; a short data entry section that can be removed from the rest of the manual; or a separate, brief data entry guide that serves to refresh memories rather than provide all the relevant information.

Questions and a rating scale for evaluating perceived ease of use of documentation manuals were developed by Dr. Frederick Bethke at IBM. Bethke wrote, "Our ultimate goal is to increase customer satisfaction, and that satisfaction is based on customers' *perception* of their own usage, not on any separate measurements."[1] Bethke's questions included the following:

1 How easy to use is this manual?

2 How accurate have you found the information in the manual to be?

3 Is this manual complete? That is, does it contain all the information it seems to promise?

4 Does this manual have extra, unnecessary information in it that gets in your way?

5 Does it require any effort to understand the language used in this manual?

6 Were you helped by the examples and figures in this manual?

7 Is the information developed in a way that makes it easy to learn?

8 Have you found any confusing or annoying inconsistencies in presentation or coverage in the manual?

9 Do you find that, when you refer to the manual, the different sections are organized logically by the kind of information they contain?

10 Do the index, the headings, the table of contents, and similar items help you ascertain where you are and how to get to specific points of information?

11 What is your opinion of the physical or aesthetic aspects of the manual?

---

[1] Dr. Frederick Bethke, International Business Machines Corporation, San Jose, Calif., published in *Technical Communication*, 1983, 2nd quarter.

12 What is your opinion of the products the manual is describing?

13 What did you like most about the manual? Least?

14 Describe in your own words the factors that are most responsible for your perceptions of the relative ease of use of the manual.

Ratings were based on a numeric scale and a descriptive scale. The numeric scale ranged from 0 to 10 with 0 denoting the most difficult-to-use manual and 10 the easiest to use. The descriptive scale offered four choices—very easy, fairly easy, fairly difficult, and very difficult. A baseline was established by evaluating 30 randomly selected manuals from the 1000 distributed; 20 users of each manual were surveyed. New manuals were then evaluated in relation to this benchmark.

Correlation tests indicated that "natural development, completeness, and logical arrangement are the qualities that show the highest degree of correlation, and hence are apparently the factors that contribute most to an overall impression of ease of use. The lowest correlations are for freedom from extraneous information, concreteness, and consistency." A correlation was noted also between the user's perception of the difficulty of the product and the difficulty of the manual.[2]

---

[2]Ibid.

EIGHT

Production Management, Procedures, and Options

The first impression of the documentation you have created is governed by production decisions. Ease of use is also a direct result of these decisions. Yet, it is one of the areas in which technical writers are least schooled. Production of manuals includes preparation of copy for printing, the actual printing or copying process, binding, and assembling the final documents. Other user materials—such as posters and three-dimensional desk aids—require preparation of copy, the actual printing or copying process, and, in some circumstances, assembly of the final product.

The primary production issues for the documentation specialist include the following:

1 Management of production

2 Selection of production process

3 Format considerations

4 Preparation of copy for production

MANAGEMENT OF PRODUCTION

Familiarity with the production process is the key to managing the production of user materials. A realistic production action plan can serve as a guide through the production process. An example of a production action plan is shown in Chapter 2. This plan is a summary of the various products for which the documentation specialist is responsible, the production and binding methods to be used, the selection of the copying process, the deliverables required for copying, a contact name and phone number for the copying source (whether in-house or an outside contractor), the date the deliverables are due for copying, and the completion date. The plan can include notes such as ordering special binders or scheduling a meeting with a book designer about the final product specifications. This plan can serve as a convenient management tool. It can be adapted to fit the specific needs of any project.

Knowing your options, schedules, and copy requirements is an essential starting point for managing document production. Production options are discussed in the next section, scheduling needs are determined by specifications for each project, and copy requirements are dictated by the production process.

Some of the decisions to make prior to actual production include the following:

1 Production method

2 Production schedule

3 Text layout on page, such as margins, offset, tabs, headers and/or footers, lines per page, page width

4 Types of artwork and their paste-up requirements

5 Reductions required

6 Paper size, weight, quality, and color

7 Binding style

8 Cover design and material

9 Type style and size

10 Ink color

11 Special requirements for title page

12 Estimated number of pages of text, front matter, artwork

13 Number of copies

One excellent source of information on production is the *Pocket Pal: A Graphic Arts Production Handbook*.[1]

---

[1]International Paper Company, New York, 1983.

SELECTION OF PRODUCTION PROCESS

There are two primary choices for producing multiple copies:

1 Photocopying

2 Offset printing

No matter which production method is selected, the original manuscript probably will be produced on a word processor. In most situations, this is the only system that makes sense with the multiple drafts and revisions required in developing documentation. Word processing systems range from a text-editing program on a microcomputer to a sophisticated combination word processor–computer graphics system that produces composed pages and communicates them directly to typesetting equipment. Cost, volume, user needs, and the final copying-printing process are the primary considerations when selecting a word processing system.

Typesetting provides the quality print image and the variation in print style in professional-looking documents. Until recently, one of the problems with using this method for user documentation was the time required to complete a job. The development of phototypesetters and improvements in electronic communication systems with typesetting equipment have shortened time requirements. Typeset copy may be photocopied or used in the offset printing process.

Photocopied Manuscript

Numerous copiers are available, from standard office-style photocopiers to production (system) copiers.

Production copiers are high speed (two copies a second is not uncommon). They collate automatically, and some automatically copy on both sides of the paper in one pass. Generally, the image quality is not as good as you would get with a good, well-maintained office-style photocopier. Production photocopiers are used for high volume, both in terms of the number of pages of the original and the number of copies of the original. An example of a production copier is the Xerox 9000 series.

Office-style photocopiers vary considerably. They are slower than production photocopiers (one copy a second is a fast system). Nevertheless, some models perform functions such as reduction, color printing, and collating. They are useful for a few copies of fairly short documents or several copies of a one- or two-page document. They rarely are the best choice for multiple copies of long documents.

Most copiers today—whether production copiers or office-style photocopiers—use the dry process for photocopying. The wet process originally made clearer copies but was expensive and difficult to use. Recent improvements in the clarity achieved by the dry process have enabled it to take over the market.

Cost, volume, quality, time, and format affect the choices for photocopying. It is useful to prepare a cost study of the options. Volume—in terms of number of pages of the original and the number of originals to be copied—is the key to determining these costs. But it must be balanced against other factors.

In addition to cost, the documentation specialist must be concerned with schedules. An inexpensive in-house copier that requires considerable staff time is not less expensive to a documentation project than paying an outside copy service with more sophisticated equipment.

The smallest standard paper size is $8\frac{1}{2}$ by 11 inches. For smaller manuals, such as $5\frac{1}{2}$ by $8\frac{1}{2}$ inches, the paper must be cut. Both time and proper cutting facilities are essential.

To properly evaluate your photocopying options, determine the range of your usual projects in terms of page size; number of pages; number of copies; and any special needs, such as colored paper or hand feeding for special artwork. Put these in a columnar format and obtain price estimates from several print and copy shops. Exhibit 8-1 is an example of this form.

When photocopying multiple copies, it is essential that the original to be photocopied is printed clearly on properly formatted pages. Do not use a dot matrix printer for printing the final copy. Be sure the paper supply is clean and the print device in excellent condition.

Offset Printing

Offset printing from typeset copy provides the most professional-looking multiple copies. Depending on the number of copies to be printed, this process may be competitive in cost with production copying. The greater the number of copies, the more cost effective offset printing is.

The most common process of offset printing (also called "offset lithography") includes the following steps:

1   Text is typeset.

2   Artwork is prepared.

3   Typeset text and artwork are used to prepare mechanicals.

4   Mechanicals are photographed.

EXHIBIT 8-1

Photocopying Costs: 100 Pages, 6 by $8\frac{1}{2}$ Inches

Characteristics	Requirements	Cost for Copies			
		500	1000	3000	5000
Print quality	Avg. Production Copier				
Paper stock	20-pound bond				
Paper color	80 pages white, 20 pages blue				
Number of special graphics	8 reduced screens				
Cutting	Yes				
Total cost					

5   The galleys (photographed mechanicals) are reviewed.

6   Thin metal or paper offset printing plates are made by placing the negatives on the plates, then exposing them to very intense light. Metal plates are generally used when more than 2000 impressions are needed.

7   The plates are developed and chemically treated.

8   The plates are attached to a cylinder, called the *plate* or *master cylinder,* on the offset press.

9   The plate cylinder is moistened so the nonprint areas will not attract ink.

10 The plate cylinder is pressed against the ink rollers.

11 The inked image on the plate cylinder is imprinted on a blanket cylinder as a reverse image.

12 The blanket cylinder prints (offsets) the ink imprint onto the paper as a positive image.

13 The pages are collated.

The paper used in an offset press may be webfed, which uses a continuous roll, or sheetfed. A webfed offset press can commonly print 1000 feet per minute.

FORMAT CONSIDERATIONS

Both photocopies and typeset printed copies require several format decisions, although there are more options with typeset copy. These decisions can be categorized as follows:

1   Layout and page design, including composition and spacing

2   Type

3   Paper

4   Binding

Layout and Page Design

The *layout* is the detailed plan you present to the compositor. The more precise it is, the better your final product will be and the less time and money will be wasted during the printing process.

Measurements for printing are in picas and points. There are 6 picas to an inch, 12 points to a pica, 72 points to an inch. Picas usually measure the length (sometimes called the "width") of a line; points measure height, usually of type. *Leading* (pronounced "ledding") is the amount of space between the top of the tallest letters of type and the bottom of the line above. The final specifications for the typesetter should include the following:

1 Line length (in picas)

2 Type size and amount of leading (in points), e.g., 12-point type with 2 points of leading, which may be written as "12/14" (the latter number represents the 12-point type plus the 2 points of leading)

3 Typeface name and number (from type selection book)

4 Type weight (such as light, medium, bold, extra bold)

5 Style (such as condensed, extra condensed, Roman, italic)

Both composition and spacing influence layout decisions. The primary elements of composition are balance, proportion, and clarity. Balance may be formal (symmetrical) or informal (asymmetrical).

Formal balance gives a more conservative image and does not hold interest for long. It is based on an imaginary vertical center line with equal parts on each side of the line. Clearly, it is an easy design element to use.

Informal balance is achieved by the unequal distribution of information on a page. It is exciting and maintains interest but may be difficult to design in an aesthetically pleasing way.

Although there are rules that govern text composition, many book designers believe that the eye is the best judge. For example, a block of centered text with the same amount of white space above and below actually will appear as if its center is located lower than the middle of the page.

The *mathematical center,* which is the point at the center of the vertical and horizontal page measurements, and the *optical center* of a page are two different lines—both of which impact composition.

Book design guidelines include the following:

1 The length of the type line should be two-thirds the width of the paper.

2 The most aesthetically pleasing offset ratios for the inside, top, outside, and bottom margins are 2:3:4:5, 2:3:4:6, and 2:3:5:6.

3 Lines should not be more than 20 picas wide; otherwise, they are difficult to read.

4   Design should be planned in units, for example, two facing pages (a *spread*) should be viewed together because they form a design unit.

5   Simplicity succeeds.

Spacing involves the following considerations:

1   Amount of space between characters (letterspace)

2   Amount of space between words

3   Amount of space between lines (leading)

Criteria for determining spacing include legibility, ease of reading, and level of emphasis. Word-processed documents to be photocopied do not have word spacing flexibility. Leading can be adjusted, however. Many word processing systems allow for $\frac{1}{4}$- and $\frac{1}{2}$-line increments. Changes should be used judiciously, usually only to emphasize headings and subheadings.

To determine the length of the entire document, count each word in each of seven lines, take the average, and multiply it by the number of lines. The lines can also be estimated by taking the average for each type of page in the document. For example, pages may be predominantly text, half text, or one or two lines of text. Take the average number of words for each type of page, then multiply it by the number of pages of that type. For straight text, there are about 200 to 250 words per $8\frac{1}{2}$- by 11-inch page, double-spaced.

Type

Selection of type is an important aspect of composition. There are basically two type forms: serif (Roman) and sans serif (Gothic). *Serif type* has a short crossline at the end of each stroke. This book is printed in a serif typeface. *Sans serif* has no crossline. Serif type is easier to read for large blocks of text. Sans serif is good for headings. Two varieties of serif (or sans serif) should not be used on the same page, although it is acceptable to use a serif and a sans serif on the same page or in the same design unit. There are additional classifications of type, such as decorative type and text letters, but they are rarely, if ever, used in technical publications.

Most typefaces come in a variety of styles, such as italic, light, regular, medium, bold, and condensed. Some typefaces have combinations of two or more type styles, such as light italic or medium condensed. Exhibit 8-2 presents a variety of type styles for one typeface.

A specific typeface is available in a font for each style and point size of the type. A *font* is the complete collection of character symbols available

EXHIBIT 8-2

Styles of One Typeface

Helvetica Light
Helvetica Light Italic
Helvetica Regular
Helvetica Regular Italic
Helvetica Medium
Helvetica Medium Italic
Helvetica Bold
Helvetica Bold Italic
Helvetica Regular Condensed
Helvetica Regular Condensed Italic

Reprinted with permission of International Paper Company, New York, New York.

for a particular typeface in a particular size and style. It often is difficult for the production novice to recognize different typefaces. The most distinctive letters are *a, e, g, p,* and *t.*

Some sophisticated typesetting equipment can vary the slant within a font so that standard and italic type styles can be produced from the same font.

Paper

Paper is categorized by grade. The most common grades for production of user manuals include the following:

1 Bond

2 Book

3 Offset

4 Cover

Paper characteristics that affect printing and appearance include the following:

1 Grain

2 Weight

3 Bulk

4 Color

Paper is easier to fold along the grain. Another characteristic is that it is stiffer with the grain. *Grain* is determined during the papermaking process. It is the direction in which the fibers are stretched to create paper.

Weight is one means by which paper is identified. It refers to the weight of a ream of the mill size for a particular grade of paper, for example, 20-pound bond. A ream is 500 sheets. Mill size varies for different grades of paper; for example, the mill size of bond is 17 by 22 inches. Therefore, if five hundred 17- by 22-inch sheets of bond weigh 20 pounds, that paper is called "20-pound bond."

Bulk refers to the number of pages per inch for a specific grade and weight. It may be expressed as a range in *pages per inch (ppi)*. For example, the bulk (or bulking) range for a 50-pound book paper may range from 310 to 800 ppi.[2] It is important to know the bulk of a paper to determine the finished thickness of a manual. This is a crucial point in the creation of user guides. If they are too large or too heavy, they are unusable.

Color affects legibility as well as general appearance. The easiest-to-read combination is black type on a soft white (yellow-white) page. This is followed by green ink on white paper, then blue ink on white paper. Color illustrations reproduce best on neutral white.

Binding

Binding is the process of assembling the printed pages into a usable document. Frequently more than one document page is printed on a sheet of paper. For example, 20-pound bond is 17 by 22 inches, which can be used for four 8½-by-11 pages. The sheet may be folded in a combination of parallel and right-angle folds. *Scoring* (making a crease) is used to facilitate folding. The folded paper, no matter how many actual pages it represents, is called a *signature*. The signatures are then collated. At this point, the order should be checked to ensure it is correct. Providing the printer with explicit instructions on the order of the pages is helpful.

There are two types of binding: (1) bookbinding and (2) pamphlet binding. Bookbinding is the most commonly used binding method for user manuals. There are three types of bookbinding: (1) mechanical, (2) perfect, and (3) edition.

---

[2]Ibid.

Mechanical binding is the most common form of bookbinding for user manuals. The pages are punched either with round or slotted holes and inserted into a ring binder or comb (spiral) binding. The advantage to this binding method is that the document can lie flat or stand upright.

Perfect binding is most commonly used in paperback books. The pages are assembled, the left side is cut, that side is roughed (similar to using sandpaper) so that the paper will hold glue, glue is applied, and the pages are attached to the cover.

Edition binding is used for hardcover books and involves sewing the folded pages (signatures), trimming the pages, rounding and gluing gauze to the backbone of the assembled pages, and attaching the cover.

Pamphlet binding may be used for some forms of user guides. Saddle stitching and side stitching are the two types of pamphlet binding. Saddle stitching is used more frequently for documentation because it enables the document to lie flat. Both types of pamphlet binding include the following steps:

1 Scoring

2 Folding

3 Collating

4 Stitching

5 Trimming

Saddle stitching is stitching through the open signatures at the fold. *Side stitching* is stitching through the closed signatures on the left side. After stitching is completed for both procedures, the paper is trimmed to the correct size. All these steps may be completed by machine.

PREPARATION OF COPY FOR PRODUCTION

Photocopied Documents

The primary requirement for photocopied manuscripts is that they be clean. The copies are exact duplicates of the original. Smudges, pencil marks, coffee stains, typos—all will be reproduced as they appear on the original. It is essential to keep the final version of the original clean. It should be kept in a protective folder with a sheet of clean paper protecting the first page. It should be kept flat—not upright—in a file drawer. Artwork should be kept separate and inserted in the proper sequence just before copying.

Because this is a photographic process, two pieces of artwork pasted close together may create a shadow in the space between the two sheets of artwork. This shadow can be avoided by increasing the space between the two pieces of artwork, filling the space with correction ink, or slightly overlapping the two sheets of artwork. Rubber cement can be invaluable in pasteup for photocopying because it is easier to remove both the rubber cement and items pasted with rubber cement from the paper.

If the manual is being automatically collated, ensure that all pages are in the correct order and facing the same direction before copying starts.

Typeset and Offset-Printed Documents

Typesetting is one means for preparing text for offset printing. Because it adds a step before the actual printing does not mean it provides another chance for editing. Changes made after typesetting are extremely costly, in terms of both time and money. Therefore, before copy is submitted for typesetting, ensure that it has completed the editing and review process and that all corrections have been made.

Use standard white paper, double-space the text, and leave wide margins. Each page should be numbered and identified. Clearly indicate whether these numbers and headings should appear in the final document or if they are for the typesetter's information only.

Preparation of art for typeset copy is more complex than for photocopies. Layouts are prepared with specific measurements for both the artwork and any headings or text included. Using this as a guide, a mechanical is prepared on a white board with everything (except halftones or full-color art) pasted in its proper position. Space for halftones or color art usually is covered with red acetate cut to size. The copy is then photographed with the acetate in place. Halftones and color art are also photographed, but separately. The negatives of these are stripped into the negative of the original, which is used for making the plate for offset printing.

In the past, it was necessary to proof the *galleys* (the typeset copy) because the copy was retyped (keystroked) onto the typesetting machine. This retyping added one more step in which errors could be made. Today electronic typesetting is common, but it requires the use of embedded codes to note typesetting instructions. Often these codes can be entered on standard word processing machines, but they must be codes established by the typesetter. Electronic communication systems enable word processing systems to communicate directly to the typesetting equipment. If the document is already coded, costs are much lower and less time is required.

NINE

Documentation as a Profession

The profession of creating user guides involves several areas of interest. These include:

1 Education and training

2 Career opportunities

3 Ethics and professional standards

EDUCATION AND TRAINING

Only in the last decade have degrees in technical writing been generally available. Likewise, only since the early 1980s have documentation courses been offered at the college and university level. Today, more schools recognize the importance of this field and are adding such courses. Nevertheless, few people are qualified to teach this subject. Therefore, students interested in such courses must investigate not only the course content but also the instructor's credentials.

The documentation field has changed radically in the past few years. Someone with twenty years of data processing experience may not be the best person from whom to learn new techniques. If possible, meet with the instructor and ask about his/her approach to user documentation. The most important considerations are the following, which outline the process for creating documentation:

1 Prepare a needs assessment as a preliminary step to developing documentation.

2 Develop a user profile.

3 Define the documentation goal or training objectives.

4 Design a project methodology based on the needs assessment, user profile, and project goal and training objectives.

5 Provide clearly understandable, accurate, easily accessible information for the target audience.

If an instructor insists that a certain style or technique is the correct way to write documentation, you should be suspicious. Each documentation project must be analyzed to determine what is correct for that particular project. The process, as just defined, is the key to producing useful documentation.

A sample course might include the following components:

1 Brief history of computer industry development and description of software types

2 Survey of documentation types (technical or development documentation, product documentation, and user guides), content, and criteria for use

3 Description of project management approach and how to conduct a use analysis (needs assessment) and user profile

4 Methods of establishing project goals, preliminary content organization, resource parameters, and a project management plan

5 Procedures for research, including techniques for reading various programming languages, interviewing technical staff, and managing research data

6 Methods of writing documentation text, including styles and formats

7 Criteria for selection and creation of graphics

8 Methods for creating on-line interactive user guides

9 Techniques for editing user guides

10 Techniques for producing user guides

11 Techniques for distributing and maintaining user guides

The most important requirement is student access to a computer and to a software program to document. Designing a manual for a target audience that needs the information is an ideal project. If such a situation can not be arranged, ensure that a practical documentation project is available for the students.

Important criteria for a class documentation project are the following:

1 The project is real, that is, it serves an existing purpose; it is not "busy" work.

2 The documentation will meet the needs of specific users.

3 A project management approach is used to create the documentation.

In other words, in courses such as this, certain concepts—such as a project management approach and a user needs assessment—cannot be taught and then not implemented in the class work. The classroom must resemble the real professional world as much as possible.

One approach is to divide the class into project teams, with each team responsible for various aspects of the manual to be produced. Each team can design their own management systems and management plan components and can present reports to the class on their decisions and progress.

In addition to college and university courses, several short courses or professional seminars on documentation writing are offered. These may be presented as national seminars in conjunction with conferences, or as professional development programs affiliated with universities. For example, the Center for Professional Development at Arizona State University in Tempe has a three-day short course entitled, "Writing Better Computer Software Documentation for Users." Many similar programs exist throughout the country.

CAREER OPPORTUNITIES

Professional documentation specialists have four options. They are as follows:

1 Working for software companies

2 Working for software publishers (who do not produce their own software)

3 Working for documentation companies

4 Working as a free-lance documentation writer

Software Companies

In-house documentation departments of software companies are the most common source of employment for documentation specialists. Frequently, you have the opportunity to establish the department. You may be the only staff member for some time. In other situations, you may be joining a company that has had a documentation department for ten or more years, with established style guides and procedures for every type of manual produced. It is important to investigate the job responsibilities thoroughly and be sure you are qualified. The two situations just described require very different skills and even types of personality, although the jobs might be described similarly in help-wanted ads.

A recent market survey completed by Technical Information Associates, Inc. (the author's Denver-based company) and ABC-Clio Information Services indicated that one of the major complaints of in-house documentation specialists is a lack of management support for their work. Inadequate budgets, impossible schedules, and low status in the company hierarchy were some of the more common complaints.

Although the industry is becoming more aware of the importance of documentation and other areas of user-system interface, many companies have not adequately integrated these ideas into company policy or procedures. Interview carefully to determine the company's policy and attitude toward documentation.

Software Publishers

In this book, the term *software publishers* refers to companies that do not write or produce software but buy existing software and serve as distributors to end users and retail outlets. The role of large-scale software publishers has become increasingly important as the software market has burgeoned.

Often these companies buy the distribution rights to packages developed by individuals or small firms. The companies then improve (or create) the user guides, package the software and guides, and sell them to end users or place them in retail outlets. There are several variations on this theme. For example, a publishing company may buy several small nonrelated, independent packages, revise them to fit a standardized format and image, and sell them directly as their own software line. Such distributors often realize the importance of good documentation because they are closer to the end user than many software writers and producers. They also realize that the better the documentation, the more packages will be sold.

Documentation Companies

There are very few professional documentation companies today. This is due partly to the newness of the field and the negative attitude of many software companies about the importance of documentation. As this attitude changes with increased competition in the software market and more discriminatory buyers, more documentation companies will be started. The advantage of working for a documentation company rather than a software company is the variety of projects on which you can work. Most software companies have a defined market, whereas documentation companies work on projects for numerous software companies. Thus you would have more diverse experience. On the other hand, if you worked for a software firm in which you were establishing the documentation department, you would have more responsibility for establishing the methodology and procedures.

Free-Lance Documentation Writing

There are many free-lance documentation writers, but few of them are trained in writing user guides. One company reported that they had hired three such individuals—one after the other—and still did not have adequate documentation. Another company hired one free-lance documentation writer and after nine months gave up because nothing had yet been written. Success stories exist, but there do not seem to be many of them.

The major problem with free-lancing is that you spend most of your time marketing your services. It may be possible to arrange a contract whereby you provide all the documentation work for one or two companies (and just hope their schedules are compatible), which would provide more time for writing and require less for selling.

The problems of free-lance documentation writing are similar to those of any free-lancer: fluctuating income; unknown income; erratic work schedules; and, at least initially, a large investment of time for a minimum number of contracts. Some people enjoy free-lancing because they can be their own bosses. Others find free-lancing is a 24-hour-a-day job that leaves them no time of their own. *The Free-Lance Writer's Survival Manual*[1] is an excellent reference even though it does not provide information about documentation per se.

---

[1]Ernie Mau, Contemporary Books, Chicago, 1981.

ETHICS AND PROFESSIONAL STANDARDS

The Society for Technical Information, which is the professional association for technical writers, editors, and graphic artists, established a code of ethics for its members that is applicable to those in the documentation field. It is called the "Code for Communicators" and is presented in Exhibit 9-1.

The first paragraph is the key to establishing an ethical foundation for creating user documentation. The documentation specialist provides the bridge between the computer system and the user. The quality of that bridge is the responsibility of the documentation specialist.

Ethics for documentation specialists involve the following:

1 Presenting accurate, clearly understood information

EXHIBIT 9-1

Code for Communicators

As a technical communicator, I am the bridge between those who create ideas and those who use them. Because I recognize that the quality of my services directly affects how well ideas are understood, I am committed to excellence in performance and the highest standards of ethical behavior.

I value the worth of the ideas I am transmitting and the cost of developing and communicating those ideas. I also value the time and effort spent by those who read or see or hear my communication.

I therefore recognize my responsibility to communicate technical information truthfully, clearly, and economically.

My commitment to professional excellence and ethical behavior means that I will

- Use language and visuals with precision.
- Prefer simple, direct expression of ideas.
- Satisfy the audience's need for information, not my own need for self-expression.
- Hold myself responsible for how well my audience understands my message.
- Respect the work of colleagues, knowing that seldom is only one communications solution right and all others wrong.
- Strive continually to improve my professional competence.
- Promote a climate that encourages the exercise of professional judgment and that attracts talented individuals to careers in technical communication.

Reprinted with permission of the Society for Technical Communication, Washington, D.C.

2 Providing truthful information, even if it is detrimental to a particular product

3 Protecting proprietary information and not revealing information to potential software competitors

The first can be accomplished by analyzing the user's needs, designing materials that meet those needs, and avoiding ambiguity and imprecise language. The second is a matter of personal integrity. It does not mean you must itemize all the functions a particular software package can not perform, but it does mean you do not minimize known problems the user may encounter or attribute characteristics to the software that it does not have.

Frequently the documentation specialist is serving as a *double-agent,* that is, someone who not only is helping to sell a product but also is creating factual, accurate, useful information about it. If you end up in this dual role, make sure you keep your priorities straight.

Occasionally, you may be asked to distort the truth. Clearly, this is a matter of personal conscience, but it is difficult to imagine a situation in which you, as a technical communicator, would cooperate with such a request.

The computer industry is particularly sensitive to the importance of not revealing proprietary information. Several substantial awards have resulted from lawsuits regarding product information that was allegedly stolen or revealed. If you work for a software distribution company, documentation company, or as a free-lance writer, it is essential that you be aware of the issue of proprietary information because you will have access to software from numerous companies. You may discuss documentation techniques you have designed for other clients, but you must not talk about the structure, source code, or design of their software.

Technical Information Associates, Inc. (TIA) includes the paragraph shown in Exhibit 9-2 in all its contracts. You may want to include it in your own.

EXHIBIT 9-2

Contract Information Regarding Proprietary Data

TIA acknowledges the exposure to proprietary information and agrees that during the terms of the Agreement or at any time thereafter, any such proprietary information will not be disclosed in any way that could injure _____. TIA reserves the right to use selected sample pages from the deliverables as work samples for potential clients. These pages will in no manner expose proprietary concepts or procedures of the software.

A

Glossary

Access: Initial logging on the computer or entry into a particular system by the user; also, the computer processing procedures for moving data to or from memory.

Acoustic Coupler: A device used when utilizing a telephone for communications between a remote terminal and a storage unit.

Address: Location of information in a memory system.

Algorithm: A procedure stated by rules listed in a sequential operational form.

Alphabetic Data: Data presented by symbols (i.e., letters) of the English language.

Alphanumeric Data: Data presented by symbols of the English alphabet, Arabic numerals, and accepted special characters.

Analog Computer: A computer that represents data in relation to a physical variable.

Applications Software: Software programs for a specific end use not related to computer processing techniques and procedures.

Array: A set (or sets) of data arranged in such a way that the computer system may read it as a set or select a single component within the set when given the correct address.

Artificial Intelligence: The use of computers for functions related to human intelligence, such as reasoning.

Assembly Language: A machine-oriented programming language.

Assembler: A computer process that translates assembly-language programs or program statements into machine-language instructions.

Asynchronous: Operating independently.

Auxiliary Storage: Storage outside the computer, e.g., on diskettes or magnetic tape.

Batch Processing: Processing several groups of records at one time; often refers to processing data on computer cards.

Baud: Unit of measurement for signaling speed based on the number of times the condition of the line changes per second.

Binary: Base-2 number system, using the numerals 0 and 1.

Bit: Binary digit; a single digit of a binary number.

Block: A group of data forming a physical record that is defined by the storage medium.

Buffer: Temporary storage used during input and/or output.

Bug: An error in a program or hardware design resulting in the system's malfunctioning.

Bus: Hardware signal wires used for communication with other devices.

Byte: Eight bits treated as one unit.

Character: A single symbol usually represented by a binary code in the computer system.

Character String: A set of characters representing a unit of data.

Compiler: Translates a source program written in a programming language into machine-readable code.

Command: A specific user procedure usually involving use of a command key on the keyboard.

Computer Graphics: A system that provides for on-line input, off-line input, and output of drawings using plotters or film recorders.

Circuit Board: A flat board, usually fiberglass, on which the microprocessor chips and other system components are set and wired.

Databank: A series of related databases; sometimes used synonomously with "database."

Database: A stored collection of data related by subject.

Debugging: The process of finding and correcting errors in computer systems.

Default: The entry option selected by the system if the user does not make an entry for that particular field.

Digital Computers: Computers that manipulate numbers that represent data. The actual technology has evolved considerably since the first digital computers in the early 1950s.

Diskette: Frequently shortened to "disk," also called a "floppy disk;" a flexible magnetic-oxide-coated storage medium for data and programs.

Data Dictionary: A table or list, by field, of data entered into a system.

Dot Matrix Printer: A printer that prints characters formed by a series of small dots; more difficult to read than a letter-quality printer.

Error Message: A system-generated message that indicates a problem which may have been caused by the user or a hardware or software malfunction.

Fault-Tolerant System: Hardware and/or software that compensates for equipment-generated problems.

Field: A group of characters that represents a unit of data; a subset of a record.

File: A group of related records treated as a unit.

File Layout: A technical description of a system's files.

Fixed-Length Record: A record that contains a specified number of characters.

Floating-Point Numbers: The value of a floating-point number is based on scientific notation, e.g., 50,000,000 is written as 00.50×10^8 with 00.50 as the mantissa and 8 the exponent. The computer memory keeps track of the mantissa and the exponent, rather than the entire number.

Format: The physical style considerations for a manual, such as use of headers, means by which instructions are presented, and page numbering system.

Graphics: Illustrations, tables, and figures used to communicate specific information.

Hard Disk: A magnetic storage medium, usually used to store programs, that is not removable from the system. It provides faster access to data and can store more data than comparably sized floppy disks.

Hardware: The physical equipment of the computer system, which may include a keyboard, screen, central processing unit, and printer.

High-Level Languages: Programming languages not related to machine code used by programmers for writing programs. High-level languages are considered easier to learn than assembly languages.

Impact Printer: A printer that makes characters on paper by metal or plastic symbols striking through an inked ribbon, such as a carbon ribbon.

Input: Data entered into a computer system. Note that "input" is not a verb.

Input-Output: The process or paths by which data is entered into a computer system and is retrieved from the computer system.

Interface: The area of communication between two aspects of a computer system, such as the user and the system or the memory and the printer.

Keyboard: One component of most computer hardware systems; used to enter data and to perform various functions; usually based on standard typewriter keys with additional function keys; may also have a number pad similar to an adding machine keyboard on one side; may be actual keys or pressure-sensitive pads.

Key Field: A data entry field that is used to identify the record; more than one key field may be used for one record.

Keypunch: A machine that punches the machine-readable holes in computer cards. Rarely used today.

Kilobyte: 1024 (or 2^{10}) bytes, although the derivation of the term indicates 1000 bytes.

Letter-Quality Printer: A printer that produces high-quality characters as opposed to a dot matrix printer; usually an impact printer.

Machine Language: The computer instructions that can be directly performed by the computer; usually in binary code.

Macro: An instruction to a computer system that contains selected predefined instruction subsets; usually used as a shortcut for commonly used sets of instructions.

Mainframe: The central processing unit of a computer; more commonly, a large-scale computer system.

Master File: A file of data that may be relatively permanent or may be used to store data that is central to use of an applications system.

Memory: The component of a computer system in which programs and data are stored.

Merge: A data processing function that combines records from two or more files to form a third file in a prescribed order.

Microchip: A small silicon chip imprinted with the integrated circuits required by a microcomputer's central processing unit.

Microcomputer: A computer system utilizing a microchip or series of microchips as integrated circuits; usually refers to a system with less memory and speed than a minicomputer or a mainframe.

Microprocessor: The central processing unit of a microcomputer; also, refers to the silicon microchip that contains the circuitry for the central processing unit of a microcomputer.

Modem: A device that is used for transmitting data directly from a computer to a peripheral, such as another computer or a printer; usually converts digital data to analog form for communication and back to digital at the receiving end.

Network: A series of related computer systems that can communicate with each other.

Noise: A disturbance in a circuit or communication line that prevents the standard flow of information.

Object Code: A program written in machine language.

Operating System: One type of systems software that controls and coordinates the hardware and applications software elements to enable a program to run on the computer.

On-Line: Working directly under the control of the computer's central processing unit; also, a user's direct interface with a computer.

Output: The data delivered by the computer. Note that "output" is not a verb.

Peripherals: A variety of devices connected to a computer's central processing unit; primarily input-output devices such as printers or modems.

Personal Computer: Usually a low-cost, small microcomputer; occasionally used to describe all microcomputers.

Pixel: The smallest, single picture element displayed on a computer screen. The smaller the pixel size, the higher quality the picture representation.

Port: The connector between the computer and any input-output devices.

Portability: Describes software that can be used on more than one type of computer system.

Program: A series of instructions for the computer to perform a specific set of tasks. One software system may comprise several programs.

Prompt: A system-generated message or a symbol displayed on the computer screen, instructing the user to enter certain data or showing where the user is in the system, such as having access to a specific disk drive.

Random Access Memory: Memory that can be read from or written to at any location, which enables high-speed access to data.

Read-Only Memory: A permanent memory area that cannot be reprogrammed; data may be accessed but not entered.

Record: A set of fields that form one related unit of data.

Report: Printed or displayed output from an applications system.

Software: The set of programs that provides instructions to the computer. There are two types: systems software and applications software.

Source Code: The program written by the programmer in any one of several programming languages, which is then processed by a compiler or an assembler to be translated into machine-readable code.

String: A sequential series of alphanumeric data.

Syntax: The standardized rules of a particular programming language.

Systems Software: The set of programs that manages the computer's data-processing capabilities.

Tape: A magnetic (or optically sensitive) coated strip of material used for data entry, storage, or output.

Telecommunications: The transfer of data using public or private telecommunications media.

Teleprocessing: The processing of data (usually from remote locations) that has been sent using telecommunications systems.

Terminal: A device or computer peripheral used for data entry and output. If it does not have its own central processing unit, it is referred to as a "dumb terminal."

Utility: A type of systems software that manages certain functions relating to the applications software.

Variable-Length Record: Describes the records within one file that may each contain a different number of characters.

Word Processing System: A computer hardware-software system specifically designed for entering and manipulating text.

B

Abbreviations and Acronyms

(Languages are noted as such, and the letters used to create the language name are capitalized.)

ACM: Association for Computing Machinery.

ADP: Automatic data processing.

AFIPS: American Federation of Information Processing Societies.

AI: Artificial intelligence.

AL: Assembly Language.

ALGOL: ALGOrithmic Language (language).

ANSI: American National Standards Institute.

APL: A Programming Language (language).

APT: Automatically Programmed Tools (language).

ASCII: American Standard Code for Information Interchange.

ASIS: American Society for Information Science.

ASM: Association for Systems Management.

BASIC: Beginners All-purpose Symbolic Instruction Code (language).

BCD: Binary-coded decimal.

BNF: Backus-Naur form.

BPI: Bits per inch.

CAD: Computer-aided design.

CAI: Computer-assisted instruction.

CAM: Computer-aided manufacturing.

CCD: Charge-coupled device.

CDC: Control Data Corporation.

CICS: Customer Information Control System.

CKD: Count-key data.

COBOL: COmmon Business Oriented Language (language).

CODASYL: Conference on Data Systems Languages.

COM: Computer output on microfiche; also, computer output on microfilm.

CMI: Computer-managed instruction.

CMOS: Complementary metal-oxide semiconductor.

CPM: Critical-path method.

CP/M: Control program for microcomputers.

CPS: Character per second.

CPU: Central processing unit.

CRT: Cathode ray tube.

CSI: Command string interpreter.

DAA: Data access arrangement.

DAC (or D to A, D/A): Digital-to-analog conversion.

DAM: Direct access method.

DAT: Dynamic-address translation.

DAX: Data acquisition and control.

DBMS: Database management system.

DDD: Direct distance dialing (networks).

DDP: Distributed data processing.

DEC: Digital Equipment Corporation.

DOS: Direct operating system; also, disk operating system.

DMA: Direct memory access.

DP: Data processing.

DPMA: Data Processing Management Association.

DSS: Decision support system.

DTL: Diode-transistor logic.

EBCDIC: Extended binary-code decimal-interchange code.

ECL: Emitter-coupled logic.

EDP: Electronic data processing.

EFTS: Electronic funds transfer systems.

FBA: Fixed-block architecture.

EOJ: End of job.

EPROM: Erasable programmable read-only memory.

FORTRAN: FORmula TRANslation (language).

GIGO: Garbage in, garbage out.

GPSS: General Purpose Systems Simulator (language).

HIPO: Hierarchical input-process-output.

HP: Hewlett-Packard Corporation.

IBM: International Business Machines Corporation.

IC: Integrated circuit.

ICCP: Institute for Certification of Computer Professionals.

IEEE: Institute of Electrical and Electronics Engineers.

IFAC: International Federation of Automatic Control.

IFIP: International Federation for Information Processing.

IMACS: International Association for Mathematics and Computers in Simulation.

I/O: Input-output.

IOCS: Input-output control system.

IOP: Input-output processor.

IPL-V: Information Processing Language V (language).

IPS: Information processing systems; also, inches per second.

ISAM: Indexed sequential access method.

ISO: International Organization for Standardization.

JCL: Job control language.

K: Kilobyte, 1024 (2^{10}) bytes.

k: 1000.

LCD: Liquid-crystal display.

LED: Light-emitting diode.

LISP: LISt Processing (language).

LSI: Large-scale integration.

MICR: Magnetic-ink computer readable.

MIPS: Million operations per second.

MIS: Management information systems.

ML: Machine language.

MODEM: Modulation-demodulation.

MOS: Metal-oxide semiconductor.

MT: Machine translation.

MTBF: Mean time between failure.

MTTR: Mean time to repair.

OCR: Optical character recognition; also, optical character reader.

OEM: Original-equipment manufacturer.

OR: Operations research.

OS: Operating system.

PDL: Program Design Language (language).

PERT: Performance evaluation and review technique.

PL/l: Programming Language One (language).

POL: Procedure-oriented language.

PROM: Programmable read-only memory.

PSE: Packet-switching exchange.

RAM: Random access memory.

RJE: Remote job entry.

ROM: Read-only memory.

RPG: Report Program Generator (language).

RPN: Reverse Polish notation.

SDLC: Synchronous data-link control.

SCS: Society for Computer Simulation.

SP: Structured programming.

STC: Society for Technical Communication.

TSS: Time-sharing system.

TTL: Transistor-transistor logic.

TTY: Teletypewriter.

UART: Universal asynchronous receiver-transmitter.

UCS: Universal character set.

UPC: Universal product code.

USART: Universal synchronous-asynchronous receiver-transmitter.

VC: Virtual circuit.

VDU: Visual-display unit.

VSAM: Virtual-storage access method.

VTAM: Virtual-telecommunications access method.

Appendix

C

Programming Languages

ADA

History: Developed over seven years for the U.S. Department of Defense (DOD) by a French team; extensive public comment provided input during the development period; *Reference Manual for the Ada Programming Language* published in 1980; ANSI standards under development.

Use: Multipurpose but designed especially for varied DOD needs, specifically to become the standard language for DOD embedded-computer applications software.

Comments: Ada was designed to provide an industry standard for DOD requirements. Although development time has been extensive, not all problems have been resolved. Nevertheless, it does have advanced features and a more developed user orientation than earlier languages. Programs are written as a series of English-like statements. Each statement may represent several machine instructions. It is based on core modules (packages) that may be combined in a variety of ways, which facilitate program development by teams, debugging, and maintenance. These packages can be compiled separately. It is a complex language requiring skilled programmers. Compilers to use Ada on a variety of hardware are being developed.

ALGOL (ALGOrithmic Language)

History: Designed by representatives of the U.S. Association for Computing Machinery and European computer societies in 1958.

Use: Designed as a machine-independent language to represent algorithms and for computation primarily for scientific and mathematical applications.

Comments: Algol has been used more extensively in Europe than in the United States. It was the first language structured by blocks. Each statement is a block, and blocks can be nested within each other. Input-output procedures and file manipulations are not as easy as in other languages, such as Fortran.

APL (A Programming Language)

History: Developed in 1962 by Kenneth E. Iverson of IBM.

Use: Multipurpose procedure-oriented language used primarily for solving scientific and mathematical problems; requires a specialized keyboard.

Comments: APL is used interactively and is built on arrays of basic data elements with a set of functions for manipulating the arrays. It requires fewer arrays (statements) to create instructions than many other languages, such as Cobol. It requires a large storage area and is considered difficult to learn.

BASIC (Beginner's All-purpose Symbolic Instruction Code)

History: Developed at Dartmouth College by John Kemeny and Thomas Kurtz in the mid-1960s.

Use: Manipulation of data and problem solving; used primarily for microcomputers.

Comments: Basic is fairly simple to learn. Each instruction is written as a single statement that must appear on a single line introduced by the line number, which must increase sequentially. It is an interactive language (the system compiles it when the program is executed). It is based on four types of instructions: input, calculation, branching or controlling, and output.

C

History: Designed by Dennis Ritchie in 1972–1973 for the DEC PDP-11.

Use: Developed for minicomputers using the Unix operating system but may be used in other environments; used primarily for writing systems software and numerical, text-editing, and database programs.

Comments: C has a fast operating speed and efficient memory requirements. It is considered fairly simple to learn and notationally efficient. It is based on a series of statements of variables and functions. Functions may not be nested; otherwise, it is a block-structure language.

COBOL (COmmon Business Oriented Langauage)

History: Developed in the late 1950s and early 1960s in an attempt to develop a machine-independent language.

Use: Multipurpose, but designed specifically for business applications.

Comments: Each program is divided into four divisions: identification, environment, data, and procedure. It uses English language words and arithmetic symbols. Punctuation symbols are used to indicate certain program functions. The basic instruction is called a "sentence," followed by a "paragraph," "section," and "division." The structure makes reading the program clear, but it is not as easy to write a Cobol program as it is to understand one. ANSI standards were established in 1970.

FORTH

History: Developed in 1973 by staff at Forth, Inc.

Use: Not a traditional programming language (the polyFORTH II system, which is the fourth generation, includes a multiprogrammed operating system, Forth language compiler, assembler, and utilities).

Comments: Forth follows the principles of structured programming. Its structure enables the programmer to define parameters for program development, which permits more flexibility in program design. It is designed for microcomputers and minicomputers. One advocate says it makes good programmers appear better, and poor programmers worse.

FORTRAN (FORmula TRANslator)

History: The oldest high-level programming language; developed in mid-1950s; standards established by ANSI in 1966.

Use: Designed for solving mathematical problems for use in science and math, although it is used for some business applications also.

Comments: The basic instruction is called a "statement." The program is based on mathematical statements that are made up of variables that are replaced by exact numerical values during calculation processing.

GPSS (General Purpose Systems Simulator)

History: Developed in 1961 by Geoffrey Gordon for IBM; specifically designed for the IBM 7090 computer; does not have ANSI standards, but IBM maintains strict control over modifications.

Use: Supports simulation programs on time-shared systems; has error-checking and tracing features and can be used for a variety of simulation models.

Comments: GPSS lacks floating-point math capability and requires lengthy computer execution times. It is based on blocks, which are equivalent to statements. Each block specification requires a symbolic location name, the operation to be performed, and the block's operands. The block diagram is like a flowchart for the system. The program starts with a definition of functions used in the simulation, block definitions, entity definitions, and control statements (which represent basic functions).

LISP (LISt Processing)

History: Developed in 1956–1958 by John McCarthy and used by the artificial intelligence project at the Massachusetts Institute for Technology.

Use: Employed extensively in artificial intelligence.

Comments: Lisp is well suited to recursive operations and is interactive for programming (the interpreter reads the statement immediately). It is based on the creation of lists and their manipulation, which gives it a flexible structure. Lisp statements are lists. List elements may have permanent or variable values.

LOGO

History: Developed at the Massachusetts Institute of Technology under the direction of Seymour Papert; a dialect of Lisp.

Use: Employed specifically for developing programs on microcomputers by untrained programmers; primary use is in schools and homes.

Comments: Logo is very easy to understand but is slow for running programs. Programs are divided into smaller components, and a named procedure is written for each component. Also, new words and concepts can be stored for future use.

PASCAL

History: Developed by Niklaus Wirth of the Technical University in Zurich, Switzerland, in 1971; based on Algol, with various refinements such as more efficient manipulation of nonnumeric data.

Use: Initially used to teach systems programming and to locate coding errors; presently used for creating structured programs.

Comments: Pascal is a block-structured language. It allows for user-defined data types and use, numerous control statements, and easy manipulation of data structures. It has better input-output procedures than Algol. It is easy to implement and has efficient memory use.

PL/I (Programming Language One)

History: Developed in 1965 by IBM; designed to combine the best features of Algol, Cobol, and Fortran.

Use: A general-purpose, multitask language for use in several applications, such as scientific and mathematical problems, data processing, and systems programming.

Comments: Draft standards were published by ANSI in 1975. PL/1 uses the syntax structure and storage allocation characteristics of Algol, the record structures and input-ouput procedures of Cobol; and the arithmetic processing of Fortran. PL/1 compilers are more expensive and complex than for Algol, Cobol, or Fortran. Also, it is a more difficult language to learn. It is based on sequential statements of an algorithm and has diverse statement types and functions.

RPG (Report Program Generator)

History: Developed by IBM.

Use: Employed in producing reports in business data processing.

Comments: RPG is a unique type of language in which the programmer essentially defines the problem and the RPG system "writes" the program. This structure makes RPG less flexible than many other languages. Programs are developed on special coding forms in a column format. The forms are used to define six types of specifications: file description, file extension, line counter, input, calculation, and output.

SNOBOL (StriNg Oriented and symBOlic Language)

History: Developed in 1962 by Bell Laboratories.

Use: Employed in text processing; useful for manipulating strings.

Comments: There are several variations including Mainbol, Spitbol, and Fasbol. It has established data types and structures and three statement types: assignment, pattern matching, and replacement. It is not in widespread use today.

D

Bibliography

Covvey, H. Dominic, and Neil Harding McAlister: *Computer Consciousness: Surviving the Automated 80s,* Addison-Wesley, Reading, Mass., 1980.
  A journey through computer hardware, software, and the workings of a computer (written for the layperson).

Dahl, O.-J., E. W. Dijkstra, and C. A. R. Hoare (eds.): *Structured Programming,* Academic Press, New York, 1972.
  The first presentation of the concept of structured programming and the importance of documentation (primarily technical documentation) for the development of effective programs. It contains the seeds of many current programming practices.

Deken, Joseph: *The Electronic Cottage: Everyday Living with Your Personal Computer in the 1980's,* William Morrow, New York, 1982.
  A guide to how computers work and what they can be used for in one's daily life. Subjects covered include computer logic; using computers for games, simulations and modeling, feedback loops, teaching and learning, communications, and household management; and computer components.

Editors of *Consumer Reports: The Illustrated Computer Dictionary,* Bantam Books, New York, 1983.
  One of several computer dictionaries. This one is designed for nontechnical people. To find the one you like best, visit a bookstore with a large computer book department and check a few listings to see if you understand the definitions.

Harper, William L.: *Data Processing Documentation: Standards, Procedures and Applications,* Prentice-Hall, Englewood Cliffs, N.J., 1982.
  A basic guide to documentation that contains information on many sound practices for documentation. It is particularly useful for information about technical documentation. It was published originally in 1973 but has recently been updated.

Helms, H. L., Jr. (ed.): *The McGraw-Hill Computer Handbook,* McGraw-Hill, New York, 1983.

A comprehensive reference text on the computer industry covering a range of topics from hardware to software. It includes information on computer structures, logic, memory elements, input-output, time-sharing, programming, languages, graphics, artificial intelligence, interfacing, and voice recognition.

Kernighan, B. W., and P. J. Paluger: *The Elements of Programming Style,* McGraw-Hill, New York, 1983.

Includes information on programming expressions, structure, errors, documentation, and structured programming techniques. It is useful for the documentation specialist involved in technical programming or who must understand the structure of various programs.

Mau, Ernie: *The Free-Lance Writer's Survival Manual,* Contemporary Books, Chicago, 1981, out of print but available from the author at 3108 South Granby Way, Aurora, Colo. 80014-3817.

Useful for free-lance documentation writers who may not be aware of the free-lance pitfalls.

Pocket Pal: A Graphic Arts Production Handbook, International Paper Company, New York, 1983.

A very useful guide for printing and production procedures and information. Available from Pocket Pal Book, Post Office Box 100, Church Street Station, New York, N.Y. 10046.

Pooley, J.: *Trade Secrets: How to Protect Your Ideas and Assets,* Osborne Books, Berkeley, Calif., 1982.

Describes relevant patent, copyright, and trade-secret information for the computer industry. It is essential for documentation specialists to understand what is protected and how to protect it.

Pressman, R. A.: *Software Engineering: A Practioner's Approach,* McGraw-Hill, New York, 1983.

Designed for the systems analyst and software engineer. This book also is an excellent reference for the documentation specialist on the planning, design, and testing of software systems. It includes a glossary of software engineering terminology.

Ralston, Anthony (ed.): *The Encyclopedia of Computer Science,* Petrocelli/Charter, New York, 1976.

A complete listing of computer science subjects competently defined.

Spencer, Donald D.: *Understanding Computers,* paperback edition, Charles Scribner's Sons, New York, 1984.

Presents a very basic introduction to computers, what they can do and how they do it. Topics include history, language, the computer problem-solving process, programming, and future developments.

Society for Technical Communication: *International Technical Communications Conference Proceedings,* Society for Technical Communication, Washington, D.C., 1981, 1982, 1983, 1984.

Contains several papers in the proceedings for the above years that would be of interest to documentation specialists.

INDEX

ABOUT THE AUTHOR

Doann Houghton-Alico, President of TIA/Technical Information Associates, Inc., Denver, developed and taught one of the first college-level courses in the United States on how to write computer-user documentation (at Metropolitan State College, Denver). She was awarded the 1983 Top Hand Award, the highest honor from the Colorado Authors' League, for technical books. TIA, the company she founded and heads, specializes in user guides for applications and systems software, the design of user-system interfaces, and training of documentation specialists.